CONTENTS

INTRODUCTION

Born in 1887 James Rogers McConnell was World War I combat pilot. He was born the son of a Judge in Chicago, Illinois and not surprisingly the legal profession was in his blood. In 1908 he entered the University of Virginia, and there he founded an "aero club," demonstrating his early enthusiasm for aviation. In 1910 McConnell left law school and, deciding against pursuing a career in law, he went to live with his family in Carthage, where he was employed as the land and industrial agent of the Seaboard Air Line Railway and secretary of the Carthage Board of Trade. He also showed an aptitude for creative writing and wrote numerous promotional pamphlets for the Sandhills area of North Carolina.

Shortly after the outbreak of war in Europe in 1914, McConnell joined the American Ambulance Corps and went to France. In a letter to a friend in 1915, he wrote: "Tomorrow I am going to the front with our squad and twelve ambulances. . . . I am having a glorious experience." He was not content to sit at peace in the wagon lines and was soon active in the very front lines where he rescued a wounded French soldier while under fire. This was only one of many similar acts which eventually won him the Croix de Guerre for conspicuous bravery.

McConnell soon developed a deep conviction that America needed to do more in the war against Germany. In order to prove his personal worth McConnell resigned from the Ambulance Corps and entered the aviation training program along with many other young Americans including Kiffin Yates Rockwell of Asheville.

On completion of this training, thirty-eight US pilots formed the famous Lafayette Escadrille. Flying Nieuport biplanes which

MILITARY HISTORY FROM PRIMARY SOURCES

RECOLLECTIONS OF THE GREAT WAR IN THE AIR

EDITED AND INTRODUCED BY BOB CARRUTHERS

Pen & Sword

This edition published in 2013 by
Pen & Sword Aviation
An imprint of
Pen & Sword Books Ltd
47 Church Street
Barnsley
South Yorkshire
S70 2AS

First published in Great Britain in 2012 in digital format by
Coda Books Ltd.

Copyright © Coda Books Ltd, 2012
Published under licence by Pen & Sword Books Ltd.

ISBN 978 1 78159 244 1

Originally published as "Flying for France With the American Escadrille at Verdun"
by James R. McConnell, Sergeant-Pilot in the French Flying Corps, by Doubleday,
Page & Company, Garden City, New York in 1917. Originally illustrated from
photographs through the kindness of Mr. Paul Rockwell.

A CIP catalogue record for this book is
available from the British Library

Printed and bound by
CPI Group (UK) Ltd, Croydon, CR0 4YY

Pen & Sword Books Ltd incorporates the Imprints of Pen & Sword Aviation, Pen &
Sword Family History, Pen & Sword Maritime, Pen & Sword Military, Pen &
Sword Discovery, Pen & Sword Politics, Pen & Sword Atlas, Pen & Sword
Archaeology, Wharncliffe Local History, Wharncliffe True Crime, Wharncliffe
Transport, Pen & Sword Select, Pen & Sword Military Classics, Leo Cooper, The
Praetorian Press, Claymore Press, Remember When, Seaforth Publishing and
Frontline Publishing

For a complete list of Pen & Sword titles please contact
PEN & SWORD BOOKS LIMITED
47 Church Street, Barnsley, South Yorkshire, S70 2AS, England
E-mail: enquiries@pen-and-sword.co.uk
Website: www.pen-and-sword.co.uk

travelled at a top speed 110 miles per hour, the pilots were considered to be the knights of the air. Operating from Luxeuil Field in eastern France, the Americans generally took off at dawn each day and clad in fur-lined outfits against the cold of their unenclosed cockpits they patrolled the skies of France alive for the sight of their enemies; their normal routine was a combat patrol lasting two hours. Armed with an unsynchronised machine gun, in the event of a dog-fight the pilot had to attempt to fire at his enemy with one hand while manoeuvring the plane with the other hand and his feet. Following the Battle of Verdun, McConnell was finally issued with a new plane on which the 500-round Vickers machine gun was synchronized with the propeller. This was the era of dog-fights high above the trenches. The "aces" of the time were those pilots who had shot down five enemy planes. Deadly pursuit, interweaving flight patterns and surprise attacks were the hallmarks of this new and deadly form of warfare.

McConnell had an exceptional command of the English language and in his surviving letters home and also in 'Flying for France', McConnell wrote powerfully what it meant to take to the air, of the sun on the fog, of silver bullets and of the red flames from the artillery below looking like a Doré painting of Dante's hell. Not surprisingly for a pilot who was so often in the thick of the fighting he was wounded once and narrowly escaping death on numerous other occasions. McConnell's luck finally ran out when he was flying in the vicinity of St Quentin, it was here that two German planes cornered him and shot him down on 19th March 1917. The plane and his body were later found by the French army and he was buried on the spot at the edge of the village of Hussy. According to one obituary, his death came "far above the smoke and filth and grime in the clear, clean air of heaven, attended by the stern joy of combat."

A monument erected to McConnell in Carthage, North Carolina bears an inscription reading in part, "He fought for

Humanity, Liberty and Democracy, lighted the way for his countrymen and showed all men how to dare nobly and to die gloriously." A statue by Gutzon Borglum adorns the grounds of the University of Virginia, with these words at the base: "Soaring like an eagle into new heavens of valour and devotion."

Thank you very much for buying this book. It tells the proud story of an amazing man. I hope it gives you as much pleasure to read as it gave me in putting it together for you.

Bob Carruthers
Nice, 2012

DEDICATION

TO

MRS. ALICE S. WEEKS

*Who having lost a splendid son in the
French Army has given to a great number of us
other Americans in the war
the tender sympathy and help of a mother.*

INTRODUCTION BY F.C.P.

One day in January, 1915, I saw Jim McConnell in front of the Court House at Carthage, North Carolina. "Well," he said, "I'm all fixed up and am leaving on Wednesday."

"Where for?" I asked.

"I've got a job to drive an ambulance in France," was his answer.

And then he went on to tell me, first, that as he saw it the greatest event in history was going on right at hand and that he would be missing the opportunity of a lifetime if he did not see it. "These Sand Hills," he said "will be here forever, but the war won't; and so I'm going." Then, as an afterthought, he added: "And I'll be of some use, too, not just a sight-seer looking on; that wouldn't be fair."

So he went. He joined the American ambulance service in the Vosges, was mentioned more than once in the orders of the day for conspicuous bravery in saving wounded under fire, and received the much-coveted Croix de Guerre.

Meanwhile, he wrote interesting letters home. And his point of view changed, even as does the point of view of all Americans who visit Europe. From the attitude of an adventurous spirit anxious to see the excitement, his letters showed a new belief that any one who goes to France and is not able and willing to do more than his share—to give everything in him toward helping the wounded and suffering—has no business there.

And as time went on, still a new note crept into his letters; the first admiration for France was strengthened and almost replaced by a new feeling—a profound conviction that France and the French people were fighting the fight of liberty against enormous odds. The new spirit of France—the spirit of the

JAMES R. McCONNELL
"I frankly confess to a feeling of marked satisfaction at receiving that
grade [Sergeant] in the world's finest army"

"Marseillaise," strengthened by a grim determination and absolute certainty of being right—pervades every line he writes. So he gave up the ambulance service and enlisted in the French flying corps along with an ever-increasing number of other Americans.

The spirit which pervades them is something above the spirit of adventure that draws many to war; it is the spirit of a man who has found an inspiring duty toward the advancement of liberty and humanity and is glad and proud to contribute what he can.

His last letters bring out a new point—the assurance of victory of a just cause. "Of late," he writes, "things are much brighter and one can feel a certain elation in the air. Victory, before, was a sort of academic certainty; now, it is felt."

F. C. P.
November 10, 1916.

CHAPTER I

VERDUN

Beneath the canvas of a huge hangar mechanicians are at work on the motor of an airplane. Outside, on the borders of an aviation field, others loiter awaiting their aerial charge's return from the sky. Near the hangar stands a hut-shaped tent. In front of it several short-winged biplanes are lined up; inside it three or four young men are lolling in wicker chairs.

They wear the uniform of French army aviators. These uniforms, and the grim-looking machine guns mounted on the upper planes of the little aircraft, are the only warlike note in a pleasantly peaceful scene. The war seems very remote. It is hard to believe that the greatest of all battles—Verdun—rages only twenty-five miles to the north, and that the field and hangars and mechanicians and aviators and airplanes are all playing a part therein.

Suddenly there is the distant hum of a motor. One of the pilots emerges from the tent and gazes fixedly up into the blue sky. He points, and one glimpses a black speck against the blue, high overhead. The sound of the motor ceases, and the speck grows larger. It moves earthward in steep dives and circles, and as it swoops closer, takes on the shape of an airplane. Now one can make out the red, white, and blue circles under the wings which mark a French war-plane, and the distinctive insignia of the pilot on its sides.

"Ton patron arrive!" one mechanician cries to another. "Your boss is coming!"

The machine dips sharply over the top of a hangar, straightens out again near the earth at a dizzy speed a few feet above it and, losing momentum in a surprisingly short time, hits the ground with tail and wheels. It bumps along a score of yards and then, its motor whirring again, turns, rolls toward the hangar, and stops. A human form, enveloped in a species of garment for all the world like a diver's suit, and further adorned with goggles and a leather hood, rises unsteadily in the cockpit, clambers awkwardly overboard and slides down to terra firma.

A group of soldiers, enjoying a brief holiday from the trenches in a cantonment near the field, straggle forward and gather timidly about the airplane, listening open-mouthed for what its rider is about to say.

"Hell!" mumbles that gentleman, as he starts divesting himself of his flying garb.

"What's wrong now?" inquires one of the tenants of the tent.

"Everything, or else I've gone nutty," is the indignant reply, delivered while disengaging a leg from its Teddy Bear trousering. "Why, I emptied my whole roller on a Boche this morning, point blank at not fifteen metres off. His machine gun quit firing and his propeller wasn't turning and yet the darn fool just hung up there as if he were tied to a cloud. Say, I was so sure I had him it made me sore—felt like running into him and yelling, 'Now, you fall, you bum!'"

The eyes of the poilus register surprise. Not a word of this dialogue, delivered in purest American, is intelligible to them. Why is an aviator in a French uniform speaking a foreign tongue, they mutually ask themselves. Finally one of them, a little chap in a uniform long since bleached of its horizon-blue colour by the mud of the firing line, whisperingly interrogates a mechanician as to the identity of these strange air folk.

"But they are the Americans, my old one," the latter explains with noticeable condescension.

Marvelling afresh, the infantrymen demand further details. They learn that they are witnessing the return of the American Escadrille—composed of Americans who have volunteered to fly for France for the duration of the war—to their station near

Bar-le-Duc, twenty-five miles south of Verdun, from a flight over the battle front of the Meuse. They have barely had time to digest this knowledge when other dots appear in the sky, and one by one turn into airplanes as they wheel downward. Finally all six of the machines that have been aloft are back on the ground and the American Escadrille has one more sortie over the German lines to its credit.

PERSONNEL OF THE ESCADRILLE

Like all worth-while institutions, the American Escadrille, of which I have the honour of being a member, was of gradual growth. When the war began, it is doubtful whether anybody anywhere envisaged the possibility of an American entering the French aviation service. Yet, by the fall of 1915, scarcely more than a year later, there were six Americans serving as full-fledged pilots, and now, in the summer of 1916, the list numbers fifteen or more, with twice that number training for their pilot's license in the military aviation schools.

The pioneer of them all was William Thaw, of Pittsburg, who is to-day the only American holding a commission in the French flying corps. Lieutenant Thaw, a flyer of considerable reputation in America before the war, had enlisted in the Foreign Legion in August, 1914. With considerable difficulty he had himself transferred, in the early part of 1915, into aviation, and the autumn of that year found him piloting a Caudron biplane, and doing excellent observation work. At the same time, Sergeants Norman Prince, of Boston, and Elliot Cowdin, of New York—who were the first to enter the aviation service coming directly from the United States—were at the front on Voisin planes with a cannon mounted in the bow.

Sergeant Bert Hall, who signs from the Lone Star State and had got himself shifted from the Foreign Legion to aviation soon after Thaw, was flying a Nieuport fighting machine, and, a little later, instructing less-advanced students of the air in the Avord Training School. His particular chum in the Foreign Legion,

Sergeant Bert Hall and his Nieuport 11

James Bach, who also had become an aviator, had the distressing distinction soon after he reached the front of becoming the first American to fall into the hands of the enemy. Going to the assistance of a companion who had broken down in landing a spy in the German lines, Bach smashed his machine against a tree. Both he and his French comrade were captured, and Bach was twice court-martialed by the Germans on suspicion of being an American franc-tireur—the penalty for which is death! He was acquitted but of course still languishes in a prison camp "somewhere in Germany." The sixth of the original sextet was Adjutant Didier Masson, who did exhibition flying in the States until—Carranza having grown ambitious in Mexico—he turned his talents to spotting los Federales for General Obregon. When the real war broke out, Masson answered the call of his French blood and was soon flying and fighting for the land of his ancestors.

Of the other members of the escadrille Sergeant Givas Lufbery, American citizen and soldier, but dweller in the world at large, was among the earliest to wear the French airman's wings. Exhibition work with a French pilot in the Far East prepared him efficiently for the task of patiently unloading explosives on to German military centres from a slow-moving Voisin which was his first mount. Upon the heels of Lufbery came two more graduates of the Foreign Legion—Kiffin Rockwell, of Asheville, N.C., who had been wounded at Carency; Victor Chapman, of New York, who after recovering from his wounds became an airplane bomb-dropper and so caught the craving to become a pilot. At about this time one Paul Pavelka, whose birthplace was Madison, Conn., and who from the age of fifteen had sailed the seven seas, managed to slip out of the Foreign Legion into aviation and joined the other Americans at Pau.

There seems to be a fascination to aviation, particularly when it is coupled with fighting. Perhaps it's because the game is new, but more probably because as a rule nobody knows anything about it. Whatever be the reason, adventurous young Americans were attracted by it in rapidly increasing numbers. Many of them, of course, never got fascinated beyond the stage of talking about joining. Among the chaps serving with the American ambulance field sections a good many imaginations were stirred, and a few actually did enlist, when, toward the end of the summer of 1915, the Ministry of War, finding that the original American pilots had made good, grew more liberal in considering applications.

Chouteau Johnson, of New York; Lawrence Rumsey, of Buffalo; Dudley Hill, of Peekskill, N.Y.; and Clyde Balsley, of El Paso; one after another doffed the ambulance driver's khaki for the horizon-blue of the French flying corps. All of them had seen plenty of action, collecting the wounded under fire, but they were all tired of being non-combatant spectators. More or less the same feeling actuated me, I suppose. I had come over from Carthage, N.C., in January, 1915, and worked with an American ambulance section in the Bois-le-Prêtre. All along I had been convinced that the United States ought to aid in the struggle against Germany. With that conviction, it was plainly up to me to do more than drive an ambulance. The more I saw the splendour of the fight the French were fighting, the more I felt like an embusqué—what the British call a "shirker." So I made up my mind to go into aviation.

A special channel had been created for the reception of applications from Americans, and my own was favourably replied to within a few days. It took four days more to pass through all the various departments, sign one's name to a few hundred papers, and undergo the physical examinations. Then I was sent to the aviation depot at Dijon and fitted out with a uniform and personal equipment. The next stop was the school at Pau, where I was to be taught to fly. My elation at arriving there was second only to my satisfaction at being a French soldier. It was a vast improvement, I thought, in the American Ambulance.

Talk about forming an all-American flying unit, or escadrille, was rife while I was at Pau. What with the pilots already breveted, and the élèves, or pupils in the training-schools, there were quite enough of our compatriots to man the dozen airplanes in one escadrille. Every day somebody "had it absolutely straight" that we were to become a unit at the front, and every other day the report turned out to be untrue. But at last, in the month of February, our dream came true. We learned that a captain had actually been assigned to command an American escadrille and that the Americans at the front had been recalled and placed under his orders. Soon afterward we élèves got another delightful thrill.

THREE TYPES OF FRENCH AIR SERVICE

Thaw, Prince, Cowdin, and the other veterans were training on the Nieuport! That meant the American Escadrille was to fly the Nieuport—the best type of avion de chasse—and hence would be a fighting unit. It is necessary to explain parenthetically here that French military aviation, generally speaking, is divided

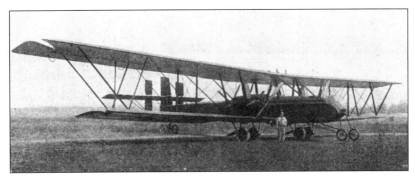
Voisin XII Bn.2

into three groups—the avions de chasse or airplanes of pursuit, which are used to hunt down enemy aircraft or to fight them off; avions de bombardement, big, unwieldy monsters for use in bombarding raids; and avions de réglage, cumbersome creatures designed to regulate artillery fire, take photographs, and do scout duty. The Nieuport is the smallest, fastest-rising, fastest-moving biplane in the French service. It can travel 110 miles an hour, and is a one-man apparatus with a machine gun mounted on its roof and fired by the pilot with one hand while with the other and his feet he operates his controls. The French call their Nieuport pilots the "aces" of the air. No wonder we were tickled to be included in that august brotherhood!

Before the American Escadrille became an established fact, Thaw and Cowdin, who had mastered the Nieuport, managed to be sent to the Verdun front. While there Cowdin was credited with having brought down a German machine and was proposed for the Médaille Militaire, the highest decoration that can be awarded a non-commissioned officer or private.

After completing his training, receiving his military pilot's brevet, and being perfected on the type of plane he is to use at the front, an aviator is ordered to the reserve headquarters near Paris to await his call. Kiffin Rockwell and Victor Chapman had been there for months, and I had just arrived, when on the 16th of April orders came for the Americans to join their escadrille at Luxeuil, in the Vosges.

Some of the Americans who are flying for France
Left to right: Victor Chapman (killed), Elliot Cowdin, Bert Hall, Lieut.
William Thaw, Capt. Thénault, Lieut. de Laage de Mux, Norman Prince
(killed), Kiffin Rockwell (killed) and James McConnell.

The rush was breathless! Never were flying clothes and fur coats drawn from the quartermaster, belongings packed, and red tape in the various administrative bureaux unfurled, with such headlong haste. In a few hours we were aboard the train, panting, but happy. Our party consisted of Sergeant Prince, and Rockwell, Chapman, and myself, who were only corporals at that time. We were joined at Luxeuil by Lieutenant Thaw and Sergeants Hall and Cowdin.

For the veterans our arrival at the front was devoid of excitement; for the three neophytes—Rockwell, Chapman, and myself—it was the beginning of a new existence, the entry into an unknown world. Of course Rockwell and Chapman had seen plenty of warfare on the ground, but warfare in the air was as novel to them as to me. For us all it contained unlimited possibilities for initiative and service to France, and for them it must have meant, too, the restoration of personality lost during those months in the trenches with the Foreign Legion. Rockwell summed it up characteristically.

"Well, we're off for the races," he remarked.

PILOT LIFE AT THE FRONT

There is a considerable change in the life of a pilot when he arrives on the front. During the training period he is subject to rules and regulations as stringent as those of the barracks. But once assigned to duty over the firing line he receives the treatment accorded an officer, no matter what his grade. Save when he is flying or on guard, his time is his own. There are no roll calls or other military frills, and in place of the bunk he slept upon as an élève, he finds a regular bed in a room to himself, and the services of an orderly. Even men of higher rank who although connected with his escadrille are not pilots, treat him with respect. His two mechanicians are under his orders. Being volunteers, we Americans are shown more than the ordinary consideration by the ever-generous French Government, which sees to it that we have the best of everything.

On our arrival at Luxeuil we were met by Captain Thénault, the French commander of the American Escadrille—officially known as No. 124, by the way—and motored to the aviation field in one of the staff cars assigned to us. I enjoyed that ride. Lolling back against the soft leather cushions, I recalled how in my apprenticeship days at Pau I had had to walk six miles for my laundry.

The equipment awaiting us at the field was even more impressive than our automobile. Everything was brand new, from the fifteen Fiat trucks to the office, magazine, and rest tents. And the men attached to the escadrille! At first sight they seemed to outnumber the Nicaraguan army—mechanicians, chauffeurs, armourers, motorcyclists, telephonists, wireless operators, Red Cross stretcher bearers, clerks! Afterward I learned they totalled seventy-odd, and that all of them were glad to be connected with the American Escadrille.

In their hangars stood our trim little Nieuports. I looked mine over with a new feeling of importance and gave orders to my mechanicians for the mere satisfaction of being able to. To find oneself the sole proprietor of a fighting airplane is quite a treat, let me tell you. One gets accustomed to it, though, after one has used up two or three of them—at the French Government's expense.

Rooms were assigned to us in a villa adjoining the famous hot baths of Luxeuil, where Caesar's cohorts were wont to besport themselves. We messed with our officers, Captain Thénault and Lieutenant de Laage de Mieux, at the best hotel in town. An automobile was always on hand to carry us to the field. I began to wonder whether I was a summer resorter instead of a soldier.

Among the pilots who had welcomed us with open arms, we discovered the famous Captain Happe, commander of the Luxeuil bombardment group. The doughty bomb-dispenser, upon whose head the Germans have set a price, was in his quarters. After we had been introduced, he pointed to eight little boxes arranged on a table.

"They contain Croix de Guerre for the families of the men I lost on my last trip," he explained, and he added: "It's a good thing you're here to go along with us for protection. There are lots of Boches in this sector."

I thought of the luxury we were enjoying: our comfortable beds, baths, and motor cars, and then I recalled the ancient custom of giving a man selected for the sacrifice a royal time of it before the appointed day.

To acquaint us with the few places where a safe landing was possible we were motored through the Vosges Mountains and on into Alsace. It was a delightful opportunity to see that glorious countryside, and we appreciated it the more because we knew its charm would be lost when we surveyed it from the sky. From the air the ground presents no scenic effects. The ravishing beauty of the Val d'Ajol, the steep mountain sides bristling with a solid mass of giant pines, the myriads of glittering cascades tumbling downward through fairylike avenues of verdure, the roaring, tossing torrent at the foot of the slope—all this loveliness, seen from an airplane at 12,000 feet, fades into flat splotches of green traced with a tiny ribbon of silver.

The American Escadrille was sent to Luxeuil primarily to acquire the team work necessary to a flying unit. Then, too, the new pilots needed a taste of anti-aircraft artillery to familiarize them with the business of aviation over a battlefield. They shot well in that sector, too. Thaw's machine was hit at an altitude of 13,000 feet.

THE ESCADRILLE'S FIRST SORTIE

The memory of the first sortie we made as an escadrille will always remain fresh in my mind because it was also my first trip over the lines. We were to leave at six in the morning. Captain Thénault pointed out on his aerial map the route we were to follow. Never having flown over this region before, I was afraid of losing myself. Therefore, as it is easier to keep other airplanes in sight when one is above them, I began climbing as rapidly as possible, meaning to trail along in the wake of my companions. Unless one has had practice in flying in formation, however, it is hard to keep in contact. The diminutive avions de chasse are

A French Caudron G.3 reconnaissance plane captured by German troops. The G.3 was used from 1914 to 1916.

the merest pinpoints against the great sweep of landscape below and the limitless heavens above. The air was misty and clouds were gathering. Ahead there seemed a barrier of them. Although as I looked down the ground showed plainly, in the distance everything was hazy. Forging up above the mist, at 7,000 feet, I lost the others altogether. Even when they are not closely joined, the clouds, seen from immediately above, appear as a solid bank of white. The spaces between are indistinguishable. It is like being in an Arctic ice field.

To the south I made out the Alps. Their glittering peaks projected up through the white sea about me like majestic icebergs. Not a single plane was visible anywhere, and I was growing very uncertain about my position. My splendid isolation had become oppressive, when, one by one, the others began bobbing up above the cloud level, and I had company again.

We were over Belfort and headed for the trench lines. The cloud banks dropped behind, and below us we saw the smiling plain of Alsace stretching eastward to the Rhine. It was distinctly pleasurable, flying over this conquered land. Following the course of the canal that runs to the Rhine, I sighted, from a height of 13,000 feet over Dannemarie, a series of brown, woodworm-like tracings on the ground—the trenches!

SHRAPNEL THAT COULDN'T BE HEARD

My attention was drawn elsewhere almost immediately, however. Two balls of black smoke had suddenly appeared close to one of the machines ahead of me, and with the same disconcerting abruptness similar balls began to dot the sky above, below, and on all sides of us. We were being shot at with shrapnel. It was interesting to watch the flash of the bursting shells, and the attendant smoke puffs—black, white, or yellow, depending on the kind of shrapnel used. The roar of the motor drowned the noise of the explosions. Strangely enough, my feelings about it were wholly impersonal.

We turned north after crossing the lines. Mulhouse seemed

just below us, and I noted with a keen sense of satisfaction our invasion of real German territory. The Rhine, too, looked delightfully accessible. As we continued northward I distinguished the twin lakes of Gérardmer sparkling in their emerald setting. Where the lines crossed the Hartmannsweilerkopf there were little spurts of brown smoke as shells burst in the trenches. One could scarcely pick out the old city of Thann from among the numerous neighbouring villages, so tiny it seemed in the valley's mouth. I had never been higher than 7,000 feet and was unaccustomed to reading country from a great altitude. It was also bitterly cold, and even in my fur-lined combination I was shivering. I noticed, too, that I had to take long, deep breaths in the rarefied atmosphere. Looking downward at a certain angle, I saw what at first I took to be a round, shimmering pool of water. It was simply the effect of the sunlight on the congealing mist. We had been keeping an eye out for German machines since leaving our lines, but none had shown up. It wasn't surprising, for we were too many.

Only four days later, however, Rockwell brought down the escadrille's first plane in his initial aerial combat. He was flying alone when, over Thann, he came upon a German on reconnaissance. He dived and the German turned toward his own lines, opening fire from a long distance. Rockwell kept straight after him. Then, closing to within thirty yards, he pressed on the release of his machine gun, and saw the enemy gunner fall backward and the pilot crumple up sideways in his seat. The plane flopped downward and crashed to earth just behind the German trenches. Swooping close to the ground Rockwell saw its débris burning away brightly. He had turned the trick with but four shots and only one German bullet had struck his Nieuport. An observation post telephoned the news before Rockwell's return, and he got a great welcome. All Luxeuil smiled upon him—particularly the girls. But he couldn't stay to enjoy his popularity. The escadrille was ordered to the sector of

The French Aviation camp near Verdun, during World War I (1916), as seen by an aviator flying at a height of 500 meters (about 1640 feet).

Verdun.

While in a way we were sorry to leave Luxeuil, we naturally didn't regret the chance to take part in the aerial activity of the world's greatest battle. The night before our departure some German aircraft destroyed four of our tractors and killed six men with bombs, but even that caused little excitement compared with going to Verdun. We would get square with the Boches over Verdun, we thought—it is impossible to chase airplanes at night, so the raiders made a safe getaway.

OFF TO VERDUN

As soon as we pilots had left in our machines, the trucks and tractors set out in convoy, carrying the men and equipment. The Nieuports carried us to our new post in a little more than an hour. We stowed them away in the hangars and went to have a look at our sleeping quarters. A commodious villa half way between the town of Bar-le-Duc and the aviation field had been assigned to us, and comforts were as plentiful as at Luxeuil.

Our really serious work had begun, however, and we knew it. Even as far behind the actual fighting as Bar-le-Duc one could sense one's proximity to a vast military operation. The endless convoys of motor trucks, the fast-flowing stream of troops, and the distressing number of ambulances brought realization of the near presence of a gigantic battle.

Within a twenty-mile radius of the Verdun front aviation camps abound. Our escadrille was listed on the schedule with the other fighting units, each of which has its specified flying hours, rotating so there is always an escadrille de chasse over the lines. A field wireless to enable us to keep track of the movements of enemy planes became part of our equipment.

Lufbery joined us a few days after our arrival. He was followed by Johnson and Balsley, who had been on the air guard over Paris. Hill and Rumsey came next, and after them Masson and Pavelka. Nieuports were supplied them from the nearest depot, and as soon as they had mounted their instruments and machine guns, they were on the job with the rest of us. Fifteen Americans are or have been members of the American Escadrille, but there have never been so many as that on duty at any one time.

BATTLES IN THE AIR

Before we were fairly settled at Bar-le-Duc, Hall brought down a German observation craft and Thaw a Fokker. Fights occurred on almost every sortie. The Germans seldom cross into our territory, unless on a bombarding jaunt, and thus practically all the fighting takes place on their side of the line. Thaw dropped his Fokker in the morning, and on the afternoon of the same day there was a big combat far behind the German trenches. Thaw was wounded in the arm, and an explosive bullet detonating on Rockwell's wind-shield tore several gashes in his face. Despite the blood which was blinding him Rockwell managed to reach an aviation field and land. Thaw, whose wound bled profusely, landed in a dazed condition just within our lines. He was too weak to walk, and French soldiers carried him to a field dressing-station, whence he was sent to Paris for further treatment. Rockwell's wounds were less serious and he insisted on flying again almost immediately.

A week or so later Chapman was wounded. Considering the number of fights he had been in and the courage with which he attacked it was a miracle he had not been hit before. He always fought against odds and far within the enemy's country. He flew more than any of us, never missing an opportunity to go up, and never coming down until his gasolene was giving out. His machine was a sieve of patched-up bullet holes. His nerve was almost superhuman and his devotion to the cause for which he fought sublime. The day he was wounded he attacked four machines. Swooping down from behind, one of them, a Fokker, riddled Chapman's plane. One bullet cut deep into his scalp, but Chapman, a master pilot, escaped from the trap, and fired several shots to show he was still safe. A stability control had been severed by a bullet. Chapman held the broken rod in one hand, managed his machine with the other, and succeeded in landing on a near-by aviation field. His wound was dressed, his machine repaired, and he immediately took the air in pursuit of some more enemies. He would take no rest, and with bandaged head continued to fly and fight.

The escadrille's next serious encounter with the foe took place a few days later. Rockwell, Balsley, Prince, and Captain Thénault were surrounded by a large number of Germans, who, circling about them, commenced firing at long range. Realizing their numerical inferiority, the Americans and their commander sought the safest way out by attacking the enemy machines nearest the French lines. Rockwell, Prince, and the captain broke through successfully, but Balsley found himself hemmed in. He attacked the German nearest him, only to receive an explosive bullet in his thigh. In trying to get away by a vertical dive his machine went into a corkscrew and swung over on its back. Extra cartridge rollers dislodged from their case hit his arms. He was tumbling straight toward the trenches, but by a supreme effort he regained control, righted the plane, and landed without disaster in a meadow just behind the firing line.

Soldiers carried him to the shelter of a near-by fort, and later he was taken to a field hospital, where he lingered for days between life and death. Ten fragments of the explosive bullet were removed from his stomach. He bore up bravely, and became the favourite of the wounded officers in whose ward he lay. When we flew over to see him they would say: Il est un brave petit gars, l'aviateur américain. [He's a brave little fellow, the American aviator.] On a shelf by his bed, done up in a handkerchief, he kept the pieces of bullet taken out of him, and under them some sheets of paper on which he was trying to write to his mother, back in El Paso.

Balsley was awarded the Médaille Militaire and the Croix de Guerre, but the honours scared him. He had seen them decorate officers in the ward before they died.

CHAPMAN'S LAST FIGHT

Then came Chapman's last fight. Before leaving, he had put two bags of oranges in his machine to take to Balsley, who liked to suck them to relieve his terrible thirst, after the day's flying was over. There was an aerial struggle against odds, far within the German lines, and Chapman, to divert their fire from his comrades, engaged several enemy airmen at once. He sent one tumbling to earth, and had forced the others off when two more swooped down upon him. Such a fight is a matter of seconds, and one cannot clearly see what passes. Lufbery and Prince, whom Chapman had defended so gallantly, regained the French lines. They told us of the combat, and we waited on the field for Chapman's return. He was always the last in, so we were not much worried. Then a pilot from another fighting escadrille telephoned us that he had seen a Nieuport falling. A little later the observer of a reconnaissance airplane called up and told us how he had witnessed Chapman's fall. The wings of the plane had buckled, and it had dropped like a stone he said.

We talked in lowered voices after that; we could read the pain in one another's eyes. If only it could have been some one else, was what we all thought, I suppose. To lose Victor was not an irreparable loss to us merely, but to France, and to the world as well. I kept thinking of him lying over there, and of the oranges he was taking to Balsley. As I left the field I caught sight of Victor's mechanician leaning against the end of our hangar. He was looking northward into the sky where his patron had vanished, and his face was very sad.

PROMOTIONS AND DECORATIONS

By this time Prince and Hall had been made adjutants, and we corporals transformed into sergeants. I frankly confess to a feeling of marked satisfaction at receiving that grade in the world's finest army. I was a far more important person, in my own estimation, than I had been as a second lieutenant in the militia at home. The next impressive event was the awarding of decorations. We had assisted at that ceremony for Cowdin at Luxeuil, but this time three of our messmates were to be honoured for the Germans they had brought down. Rockwell and Hall received the Médaille Militaire and the Croix de Guerre, and Thaw, being a lieutenant, the Légion d'honneur and another "palm" for the ribbon of the Croix de Guerre he had won previously. Thaw, who came up from Paris specially for the presentation, still carried his arm in a sling.

There were also decorations for Chapman, but poor Victor, who so often had been cited in the Orders of the Day, was not on hand to receive them.

THE MORNING SORTIE

Our daily routine goes on with little change. Whenever the weather permits—that is, when it isn't raining, and the clouds aren't too low—we fly over the Verdun battlefield at the hours dictated by General Headquarters. As a rule the most successful sorties are those in the early morning.

Norman Prince, of Boston, Mass., of the French Flying Service, who was killed flying for France

We are called while it's still dark. Sleepily I try to reconcile the French orderly's muttered, C'est l'heure, monsieur, that rouses me from slumber, with the strictly American words and music of "When That Midnight Choo Choo Leaves for Alabam'" warbled by a particularly wide-awake pilot in the next room. A few minutes later, having swallowed some coffee, we motor to the field. The east is turning gray as the hangar curtains are drawn apart and our machines trundled out by the mechanicians. All the pilots whose planes are in commission—save those remaining behind on guard—prepare to leave. We average from four to six on a sortie, unless too many flights have been ordered for that day, in which case only two or three go out at a time.

Now the east is pink, and overhead the sky has changed from gray to pale blue. It is light enough to fly. We don our fur-lined shoes and combinations and adjust the leather flying hoods and goggles. A good deal of conversation occurs—perhaps because, once aloft, there's nobody to talk to.

A German Friedrichshafen G.V bomber

"Eh, you," one pilot cries jokingly to another, "I hope some Boche just ruins you this morning, so I won't have to pay you the fifty francs you won from me last night!"

This financial reference concerns a poker game.

"You do, do you?" replies the other as he swings into his machine. "Well, I'd be glad to pass up the fifty to see you landed by the Boches. You'd make a fine sight walking down the street of some German town in those wooden shoes and pyjama pants. Why don't you dress yourself? Don't you know an aviator's supposed to look chic?"

A sartorial eccentricity on the part of one of our colleagues is here referred to.

GETTING UNDER WAY

The raillery is silenced by a deafening roar as the motors are tested. Quiet is briefly restored, only to be broken by a series of rapid explosions incidental to the trying out of machine guns. You loudly inquire at what altitude we are to meet above the field.

"Fifteen hundred metres—go ahead!" comes an answering yell.

Essence et gaz! [Oil and gas!] you call to your mechanician, adjusting your gasolene and air throttles while he grips the propeller.

Contact! he shrieks, and Contact! you reply. You snap on the switch, he spins the propeller, and the motor takes. Drawing forward out of line, you put on full power, race across the grass and take the air. The ground drops as the hood slants up before you and you seem to be going more and more slowly as you rise. At a great height you hardly realize you are moving. You glance at the clock to note the time of your departure, and at the oil gauge to see its throb. The altimeter registers 650 feet. You turn and look back at the field below and see others leaving.

In three minutes you are at about 4,000 feet. You have been making wide circles over the field and watching the other machines. At 4,500 feet you throttle down and wait on that level for your companions to catch up. Soon the escadrille is bunched and off for the lines. You begin climbing again, gulping to clear your ears in the changing pressure. Surveying the other machines, you recognize the pilot of each by the marks on its side—or by the way he flies. The distinguishing marks of the Nieuports are various and sometimes amusing. Bert Hall, for instance, has BERT painted on the left side of his plane and the same word reversed (as if spelled backward with the left hand) on the right—so an aviator passing him on that side at great speed will be able to read the name without difficulty, he says!

The country below has changed into a flat surface of varicoloured figures. Woods are irregular blocks of dark green, like daubs of ink spilled on a table; fields are geometrical designs of different shades of green and brown, forming in composite an ultra-cubist painting; roads are thin white lines, each with its distinctive windings and crossings—from which you determine your location. The higher you are the easier it is to read.

In about ten minutes you see the Meuse sparkling in the morning light, and on either side the long line of sausage-shaped observation balloons far below you. Red-roofed Verdun springs into view just beyond. There are spots in it where no red shows and you know what has happened there. In the green pasture land bordering the town, round flecks of brown indicate the shell holes. You cross the Meuse.

VERDUN, SEEN FROM THE SKY

Immediately east and north of Verdun there lies a broad, brown band. From the Woevre plain it runs westward to the "S" bend in the Meuse, and on the left bank of that famous stream continues on into the Argonne Forest. Peaceful fields and farms and villages adorned that landscape a few months ago—when there was no Battle of Verdun. Now there is only that sinister brown belt, a strip of murdered Nature. It seems to belong to another world. Every sign of humanity has been swept away. The woods and roads have vanished like chalk wiped from a blackboard; of the villages nothing remains but gray smears where stone walls have tumbled together. The great forts of Douaumont and Vaux are outlined faintly, like the tracings of a finger in wet sand. One cannot distinguish any one shell crater, as one can on the pockmarked fields on either side. On the brown band the indentations are so closely interlocked that they blend into a confused mass of troubled earth. Of the trenches only broken, half-obliterated links are visible.

Columns of muddy smoke spurt up continually as high explosives tear deeper into this ulcered area. During heavy bombardment and attacks I have seen shells falling like rain. The countless towers of smoke remind one of Gustave Doré's picture of the fiery tombs of the arch-heretics in Dante's "Hell." A smoky pall covers the sector under fire, rising so high that at a height of 1,000 feet one is enveloped in its mist-like fumes. Now and then monster projectiles hurtling through the air close by leave one's plane rocking violently in their wake. Airplanes have been cut in two by them.

THE ROAR OF BATTLE—UNHEARD

For us the battle passes in silence, the noise of one's motor deadening all other sounds. In the green patches behind the brown belt myriads of tiny flashes tell where the guns are hidden; and those flashes, and the smoke of bursting shells, are all we see of the fighting. It is a weird combination of stillness

32

World War I US Army Air Service recruiting poster

and havoc, the Verdun conflict viewed from the sky.

Far below us, the observation and range-finding planes circle over the trenches like gliding gulls. At a feeble altitude they follow the attacking infantrymen and flash back wireless reports of the engagement. Only through them can communication be maintained when, under the barrier fire, wires from the front lines are cut. Sometimes it falls to our lot to guard these machines from Germans eager to swoop down on their backs. Sailing about high above a busy flock of them makes one feel like an old mother hen protecting her chicks.

"NAVIGATING" IN A SEA OF CLOUDS

The pilot of an avion de chasse must not concern himself with the ground, which to him is useful only for learning his whereabouts. The earth is all-important to the men in the observation, artillery-regulating, and bombardment machines, but the fighting aviator has an entirely different sphere. His domain is the blue heavens, the glistening rolls of clouds below the fleecy banks towering above, the vague aerial horizon, and he must watch it as carefully as a navigator watches the storm-tossed sea.

On days when the clouds form almost a solid flooring, one feels very much at sea, and wonders if one is in the navy instead of aviation. The diminutive Nieuports skirt the white expanse like torpedo boats in an arctic sea, and sometimes, far across the cloud-waves, one sights an enemy escadrille, moving as a fleet.

Principally our work consists of keeping German airmen away from our lines, and in attacking them when opportunity offers. We traverse the brown band and enter enemy territory to the accompaniment of an antiaircraft cannonade. Most of the shots are wild, however, and we pay little attention to them. When the shrapnel comes uncomfortably close, one shifts position slightly to evade the range. One glances up to see if there is another machine higher than one's own. Low and far within the German lines are several enemy planes, a dull white

RESERVES CROSSING A RIVER ON THE WAY TO VERDUN.
"They shall not pass" is a phrase which for all time will be associated with
the heroic defense of Verdun. To future generations of French people it will
bring a thrill of pride even surpassing that enkindled by the glorious "The
Old Guard dies, it never surrenders." The guardians of the great fortress
on the Meuse have proved themselves invincible in attack, invulnerable in
defense. National Geographic Maagazine, 1917.

in appearance, resembling sand flies against the mottled earth. High above them one glimpses the mosquito-like forms of two Fokkers. Away off to one side white shrapnel puffs are vaguely visible, perhaps directed against a German crossing the lines. We approach the enemy machines ahead, only to find them slanting at a rapid rate into their own country. High above them lurks a protection plane. The man doing the "ceiling work," as it is called, will look after him for us.

TACTICS OF AN AIR BATTLE

Getting started is the hardest part of an attack. Once you have begun diving you're all right. The pilot just ahead turns tail up like a trout dropping back to water, and swoops down in irregular curves and circles. You follow at an angle so steep your feet seem to be holding you back in your seat. Now the black Maltese

Gervais Raoul Lufbery (1885-1918)

crosses on the German's wings stand out clearly. You think of him as some sort of big bug. Then you hear the rapid tut-tut-tut of his machine gun. The man that dived ahead of you becomes mixed up with the topmost German. He is so close it looks as if he had hit the enemy machine. You hear the staccato barking of his mitrailleuse and see him pass from under the German's tail.

The rattle of the gun that is aimed at you leaves you undisturbed. Only when the bullets pierce the wings a few feet off do you become uncomfortable. You see the gunner crouched down behind his weapon, but you aim at where the pilot ought to be—there are two men aboard the German craft—and press on the release hard. Your mitrailleuse hammers out a stream of bullets as you pass over and dive, nose down, to get out of range. Then, hopefully, you re-dress and look back at the foe. He ought to be dropping earthward at several miles a minute. As a matter of fact, however, he is sailing serenely on. They have an annoying habit of doing that, these Boches.

Rockwell, who attacked so often that he has lost all count, and who shoves his machine gun fairly in the faces of the Germans, used to swear their planes were armoured. Lieutenant de Laage, whose list of combats is equally extensive, has brought down only one. Hall, with three machines to his credit, has had more luck. Lufbery, who evidently has evolved a secret formula, has dropped four, according to official statistics, since his arrival on the Verdun front. Four "palms"—the record for the escadrille, glitter upon the ribbon of the Croix de Guerre accompanying his Médaille Militaire. *[Footnote: This book was written in the fall of 1915. Since that time many additional machines have been credited to the American flyers.]*

A pilot seldom has the satisfaction of beholding the result of his bull's-eye bullet. Rarely—so difficult it is to follow the turnings and twistings of the dropping plane—does he see his fallen foe strike the ground. Lufbery's last direct hit was an exception, for he followed all that took place from a balcony seat. I myself was in the "nigger-heaven," so I know. We had set out on a sortie together just before noon, one August day, and for the first time on such an occasion had lost each other over the lines. Seeing no Germans, I passed my time hovering over the French observation machines. Lufbery found one, however, and promptly brought it down. Just then I chanced to make a southward turn, and caught sight of an airplane falling out of the sky into the German lines.

As it turned over, it showed its white belly for an instant, then seemed to straighten out, and planed downward in big zigzags. The pilot must have gripped his controls even in death, for his craft did not tumble as most do. It passed between my line of vision and a wood, into which it disappeared. Just as I was going down to find out where it landed, I saw it again skimming across a field, and heading straight for the brown band beneath me. It was outlined against the shell-racked earth like a tiny insect, until just northwest of Fort Douaumont it crashed down upon the battlefield. A sheet of flame and smoke shot up from the tangled wreckage. For a moment or two I watched it burn; then I went back to the observation machines.

I thought Lufbery would show up and point to where the German had fallen. He failed to appear, and I began to be afraid it was he whom I had seen come down, instead of an enemy. I spent a worried hour before my return homeward. After getting back I learned that Lufbery was quite safe, having hurried in after the fight to report the destruction of his adversary before somebody else claimed him, which is only too frequently the case. Observation posts, however, confirmed Lufbery's story, and he was of course very much delighted. Nevertheless, at luncheon, I heard him murmuring, half to himself: "Those poor fellows."

The German machine gun operator, having probably escaped death in the air, must have had a hideous descent. Lufbery told us he had seen the whole thing, spiralling down after the

German. He said he thought the German pilot must be a novice, judging from his manoeuvres. It occurred to me that he might have been making his first flight over the lines, doubtless full of enthusiasm about his career. Perhaps, dreaming of the Iron Cross and his Gretchen, he took a chance—and then swift death and a grave in the shell-strewn soil of Douaumont.

Generally the escadrille is relieved by another fighting unit after two hours over the lines. We turn homeward, and soon the hangars of our field loom up in the distance. Sometimes I've been mighty glad to see them and not infrequently I've concluded the pleasantest part of flying is just after a good landing. Getting home after a sortie, we usually go into the rest tent, and talk over the morning's work. Then some of us lie down for a nap, while others play cards or read. After luncheon we go to the field again, and the man on guard gets his chance to eat. If the morning sortie has been an early one, we go up again about one o'clock in the afternoon. We are home again in two hours and after that two or three energetic pilots may make a third trip over the lines. The rest wait around ready to take the air if an enemy bombardment group ventures to visit our territory—as it has done more than once over Bar-le-Duc. False alarms are plentiful, and we spend many hours aloft squinting at an empty sky.

PRINCE'S AERIAL FIREWORKS

Now and then one of us will get ambitious to do something on his own account. Not long ago Norman Prince became obsessed with the idea of bringing down a German "sausage," as observation balloons are called. He had a special device mounted on his Nieuport for setting fire to the aerial frankfurters. Thus equipped he resembled an advance agent for Payne's fireworks more than an aviateur de chasse. Having carefully mapped the enemy "sausages," he would sally forth in hot pursuit whenever one was signalled at a respectable height. Poor Norman had a terrible time of it! Sometimes the reported "sausages" were not there when he arrived, and sometimes there was a super-abundancy of German airplanes on guard.

He stuck to it, however, and finally his appetite for "sausage" was satisfied. He found one just where it ought to be, swooped down upon it, and let off his fireworks with all the gusto of an American boy on the Fourth of July. When he looked again, the balloon had vanished. Prince's performance isn't so easy as it sounds, by the way. If, after the long dive necessary to turn the trick successfully, his motor had failed to retake, he would have fallen into the hands of the Germans.

After dark, when flying is over for the day, we go down to the villa for dinner. Usually we have two or three French officers dining with us besides our own captain and lieutenant, and so the table talk is a mixture of French and English. It's seldom we discuss the war in general. Mostly the conversation revolves about our own sphere, for just as in the navy the sea is the favourite topic, and in the army the trenches, so with us it is aviation. Our knowledge about the military operations is scant. We haven't the remotest idea as to what has taken place on the battlefield—even though we've been flying over it during an attack—until we read the papers; and they don't tell us much.

Frequently pilots from other escadrilles will be our guests in passing through our sector, and through these visitations we keep in touch with the aerial news of the day, and with our friends along the front. Gradually we have come to know a great number of pilotes de chasse. We hear that so-&-so has been killed, that some one else has brought down a Boche and that still another is a prisoner.

We don't always talk aviation, however. In the course of dinner almost any subject may be touched upon, and with our cosmopolitan crowd one can readily imagine the scope of the conversation. A Burton Holmes lecture is weak and watery compared to the travel stories we listen to. Were O. Henry alive, he could find material for a hundred new yarns, and William

A line up of Nieuport aircraft on a snow-covered airfield in France.

James numerous pointers for another work on psychology, while De Quincey might multiply his dreams ad infinitum. Doubtless alienists as well as fiction writers would find us worth studying. In France there's a saying that to be an aviator one must be a bit "off."

After dinner the same scene invariably repeats itself, over the coffee in the "next room." At the big table several sportive souls start a poker game, while at a smaller one two sedate spirits wrap themselves in the intricacies of chess. Captain Thénault labours away at the messroom piano, or in lighter mood plays with Fram, his police dog. A phonograph grinds out the ancient query "Who Paid the Rent for Mrs. Rip Van Winkle?" or some other ragtime ditty. It is barely nine, however, when the movement in the direction of bed begins.

A few of us remain behind a little while, and the talk becomes more personal and more sincere. Only on such intimate occasions, I think, have I ever heard death discussed. Certainly we are not indifferent to it. Not many nights ago one of the pilots remarked in a tired way:

"Know what I want? Just six months of freedom to go where and do what I like. In that time I'd get everything I wanted out of life, and be perfectly willing to come back and be killed."

Then another, who was about to receive 2,000 francs from the American committee that aids us, as a reward for his many citations, chimed in.

"Well, I didn't care much before," he confessed, "but now with this money coming in I don't want to die until I've had the fun of spending it."

So saying, he yawned and went up to bed.

CHAPTER II
VERDUN TO THE SOMME

On the 12th of October, twenty small airplanes flying in a V formation, at such a height they resembled a flock of geese, crossed the river Rhine, where it skirts the plains of Alsace, and, turning north, headed for the famous Mauser works at Oberndorf. Following in their wake was an equal number of larger machines, and above these darted and circled swift fighting planes. The first group of aircraft was flown by British pilots, the second by French and three of the fighting planes by Americans in the French Aviation Division. It was a cosmopolitan collection that effected that successful raid.

We American pilots, who are grouped into one escadrille, had been fighting above the battlefield of Verdun from the 20th of May until orders came the middle of September for us to leave our airplanes, for a unit that would replace us, and to report at Le Bourget, the great Paris aviation centre.

The mechanics and the rest of the personnel left, as usual, in the escadrille's trucks with the material. For once the pilots did not take the aerial route but they boarded the Paris express at Bar-le-Duc with all the enthusiasm of schoolboys off for a vacation. They were to have a week in the capital! Where they were to go after that they did not know, but presumed it would be the Somme. As a matter of fact the escadrille was to be sent to Luxeuil in the Vosges to take part in the Mauser raid.

Besides Captain Thénault and Lieutenant de Laage de Mieux, our French officers, the following American pilots were in the escadrille at this time: Lieutenant Thaw, who had returned to the front, even though his wounded arm had not entirely healed; Adjutants Norman Prince, Hall, Lufbery, and Masson; and

Sergeants Kiffin Rockwell, Hill, Pavelka, Johnson, and Rumsey. I had been sent to a hospital at the end of August, because of a lame back resulting from a smash up in landing, and couldn't follow the escadrille until later.

Every aviation unit boasts several mascots. Dogs of every description are to be seen around the camps, but the Americans managed, during their stay in Paris, to add to their menagerie by the acquisition of a lion cub named "Whiskey." The little chap had been born on a boat crossing from Africa and was advertised for sale in France. Some of the American pilots chipped in and bought him. He was a cute, bright-eyed baby lion who tried to roar in a most threatening manner but who was blissfully content the moment one gave him one's finger to suck. "Whiskey" got a good view of Paris during the few days he was there, for some one in the crowd was always borrowing him to take him some place. He, like most lions in captivity, became acquainted with bars, but the sort "Whiskey" saw were not for purposes of confinement.

The orders came directing the escadrille to Luxeuil and bidding farewell to gay "Paree" the men boarded the Belfort train with bag and baggage—and the lion. Lions, it developed, were not allowed in passenger coaches. The conductor was assured that "Whiskey" was quite harmless and was going to overlook the rules when the cub began to roar and tried to get at the railwayman's finger. That settled it, so two of the men had to stay behind in order to crate up "Whiskey" and take him along the next day.

The escadrille was joined in Paris by Robert Rockwell, of Cincinnati, who had finished his training as a pilot, and was waiting at the Reserve (Robert Rockwell had gone to France to work as a surgeon in one of the American war hospitals. He disliked remaining in the rear and eventually enlisted in aviation).

The period of training for a pilot, especially for one who is to

44

"Whiskey"
The lion and mascot of the American flying squadron in France.

fly a fighting machine at the front, has been very much prolonged. It is no longer sufficient that he learns to fly and to master various types of machines. He now completes his training in schools where aerial shooting is taught, and in others where he practises combat, group manoeuvres, and acrobatic stunts such as looping the loop and the more difficult tricks. In all it requires from seven to nine months.

Dennis Dowd, of Brooklyn, N.Y., is so far the only American volunteer aviator killed while in training. Dowd, who had joined the Foreign Legion, shortly after the war broke out, was painfully wounded during the offensive in Champagne. After his recovery he was transferred, at his request, into aviation. At the Buc school he stood at the head of the fifteen Americans who were learning to be aviators, and was considered one of the most promising pilots in the training camp. On August 11, 1916, while making a flight preliminary to his brevet, Dowd fell from a height of only 260 feet and was instantly killed. Either he had fainted or a control had broken.

While a patient at the hospital Dowd had been sent packages by a young French girl of Neuilly. A correspondence ensued, and when Dowd went to Paris on convalescent leave he and the young lady became engaged. He was killed just before the time set for the wedding.

When the escadrille arrived at Luxeuil it found a great surprise in the form of a large British aviation contingent. This detachment from the Royal Navy Flying Corps numbered more than fifty pilots and a thousand men. New hangars harboured their fleet of bombardment machines. Their own anti-aircraft batteries were in emplacements near the field. Though detached from the British forces and under French command this unit followed the rule of His Majesty's armies in France by receiving all of its food and supplies from England. It had its own transport service.

Our escadrille had been in Luxeuil during the months of April and May. We had made many friends amongst the townspeople and the French pilots stationed there, so the older members of the American unit were welcomed with open arms and their new comrades made to feel at home in the quaint Vosges town. It wasn't long, however, before the Americans and the British got together. At first there was a feeling of reserve on both sides but once acquainted they became fast friends. The naval pilots were quite representative of the United Kingdom hailing as they did from England, Canada, New South Wales, South Africa, and other parts of the Empire. Most of them were soldiers by profession. All were officers, but they were as democratic as it is possible to be. As a result there was a continuous exchange of dinners. In a few days every one in this Anglo-American alliance was calling each other by some nickname and swearing lifelong friendship.

"We didn't know what you Yanks would be like," remarked one of the Englishmen one day. "Thought you might be snobby on account of being volunteers, but I swear you're a bloody human lot." That, I will explain, is a very fine compliment.

There was trouble getting new airplanes for every one in the escadrille. Only five arrived. They were the new model Nieuport fighting machine. Instead of having only 140 square feet of supporting surface, they had 160, and the forty-seven shot Lewis machine gun had been replaced by the Vickers, which fires five hundred rounds. This gun is mounted on the hood and by means of a timing gear shoots through the propeller. The 160 foot Nieuport mounts at a terrific rate, rising to 7,000 feet in six minutes. It will go to 20,000 feet handled by a skillful pilot.

It was some time before these airplanes arrived and every one was idle. There was nothing to do but loaf around the hotel, where the American pilots were quartered, visit the British in their barracks at the field, or go walking. It was about as much like war as a Bryan lecture. While I was in the hospital I received a letter written at this time from one of the boys. I opened it

French soldiers of the 87th Regiment, 6th Division, at Côte 304, (Hill 304), northwest of Verdun, 1916.

expecting to read of an air combat. It informed me that Thaw had caught a trout three feet long, and that Lufbery had picked two baskets of mushrooms.

Day after day the British planes practised formation flying. The regularity with which the squadron's machines would leave the ground was remarkable. The twenty Sopwiths took the air at precise intervals, flew together in a V formation while executing difficult manoeuvres, and landed one after the other with the exactness of clockwork. The French pilots flew the Farman and Breguet bombardment machines whenever the weather permitted. Every one knew some big bombardment was ahead but when it would be made or what place was to be attacked was a secret.

Considering the number of machines that were continually roaring above the field at Luxeuil it is remarkable that only two fatal accidents occurred. One was when a British pilot tried diving at a target, for machine-gun practice, and was unable to redress his airplane. Both he and his gunner were killed. In the second accident I lost a good friend—a young Frenchman. He took up his gunner in a two-seated Nieuport. A young Canadian pilot accompanied by a French officer followed in a Sopwith. When at about a thousand feet they began to manoeuvre about one another. In making a turn too close the tips of their wings touched. The Nieuport turned downward, its wings folded, and it fell like a stone. The Sopwith fluttered a second or two, then its wings buckled and it dropped in the wake of the Nieuport. The two men in each of the planes were killed outright.

Next to falling in flames a drop in a wrecked machine is the worst death an aviator can meet. I know of no sound more horrible than that made by an airplane crashing to earth. Breathless one has watched the uncontrolled apparatus tumble through the air. The agony felt by the pilot and passenger seems to transmit itself to you. You are helpless to avert the certain death. You cannot even turn your eyes away at the moment of impact. In the dull, grinding crash there is the sound of breaking bones.

Luxeuil was an excellent place to observe the difference that exists between the French, English, and American aviator, but when all is said and done there is but little difference. The Frenchman is the most natural pilot and the most adroit. Flying comes easier to him than to an Englishman or American, but once accustomed to an airplane and the air they all accomplish the same amount of work. A Frenchman goes about it with a little more dash than the others, and puts on a few extra frills, but the Englishman calmly carries out his mission and obtains the same results. An American is a combination of the two, but neither better nor worse. Though there is a large number of expert German airmen I do not believe the average Teuton makes as good a flier as a Frenchman, Englishman, or American.

In spite of their bombardment of open towns and the use of explosive bullets in their aerial machine guns, the Boches have shown up in a better light in aviation than in any other arm. A few of the Hun pilots have evinced certain elements of honor and decency. I remember one chap that was the right sort.

He was a young man but a pilot of long standing. An old infantry captain stationed near his aviation field at Etain, east of Verdun, prevailed upon this German pilot to take him on a flight. There was a new machine to test out and he told the captain to climb aboard. Foolishly he crossed the trench lines and, actuated by a desire to give his passenger an interesting trip, proceeded to fly over the French aviation headquarters. Unfortunately for him he encountered three French fighting planes which promptly opened fire. The German pilot was wounded in the leg and the gasoline tank of his airplane was pierced. Under him was an aviation field. He decided to land. The machine was captured before the Germans had time to burn it up. Explosive bullets were discovered in the machine gun. A French officer turned to the German captain and informed him that he would probably be shot for using explosive bullets. The captain did not understand.

"Don't shoot him," said the pilot, using excellent French, "if you're going to shoot any one take me. The captain has nothing to do with the bullets. He doesn't even know how to work a machine gun. It's his first trip in an airplane."

"Well, if you'll give us some good information, we won't shoot you," said the French officer.

General view of the battlefield of Beaumont Hamel in the Somme showing the blasted land, November 1916

"Information," replied the German, "I can't give you any. I come from Etain, and you know where that is as well as I do."

"No, you must give us some worth-while information, or I'm afraid you'll be shot," insisted the Frenchman.

"If I give you worth-while information," answered the pilot, "you'll go over and kill a lot of soldiers, and if I don't you'll only kill one—so go ahead."

The last time I heard of the Boche he was being well taken care of.

Kiffin Rockwell and Lufbery were the first to get their new machines ready and on the 23rd of September went out for the first flight since the escadrille had arrived at Luxeuil. They became separated in the air but each flew on alone, which was a dangerous thing to do in the Alsace sector. There is but little fighting in the trenches there, but great air activity. Due to the British and French squadrons at Luxeuil, and the threat their presence implied, the Germans had to oppose them by a large fleet of fighting machines. I believe there were more than forty

Fokkers alone in the camps of Colmar and Habsheim. Observation machines protected by two or three fighting planes would venture far into our lines. It is something the Germans dare not do on any other part of the front. They had a special trick that consisted in sending a large, slow observation machine into our lines to invite attack. When a French plane would dive after it, two Fokkers, that had been hovering high overhead, would drop on the tail of the Frenchman and he stood but small chance if caught in the trap.

Just before Kiffin Rockwell reached the lines he spied a German machine under him flying at 11,000 feet. I can imagine the satisfaction he felt in at last catching an enemy plane in our lines. Rockwell had fought more combats than the rest of us put together, and had shot down many German machines that had fallen in their lines, but this was the first time he had had an opportunity of bringing down a Boche in our territory.

A captain, the commandant of an Alsatian village, watched the aerial battle through his field glasses. He said that Rockwell approached so close to the enemy that he thought there would be a collision. The German craft, which carried two machine guns, had opened a rapid fire when Rockwell started his dive. He plunged through the stream of lead and only when very close to his enemy did he begin shooting. For a second it looked as though the German was falling, so the captain said, but then he saw the French machine turn rapidly nose down, the wings of one side broke off and fluttered in the wake of the airplane, which hurtled earthward in a rapid drop. It crashed into the ground in a small field—a field of flowers—a few hundred yards back of the trenches. It was not more than two and a half miles from the spot where Rockwell, in the month of May, brought down his first enemy machine. The Germans immediately opened up on the wreck with artillery fire. In spite of the bursting shrapnel, gunners from a near-by battery rushed out and recovered poor Rockwell's broken body. There was a hideous wound in his breast where an explosive bullet had torn through. A surgeon who examined the body, testified that if it had been an ordinary bullet Rockwell would have had an even chance of landing with only a bad wound. As it was he was killed the instant the unlawful missile exploded.

Lufbery engaged a German craft but before he could get to close range two Fokkers swooped down from behind and filled his aeroplane full of holes. Exhausting his ammunition he landed at Fontaine, an aviation field near the lines. There he learned of Rockwell's death and was told that two other French machines had been brought down within the hour. He ordered his gasoline tank filled, procured a full band of cartridges and soared up into the air to avenge his comrade. He sped up and down the lines, and made a wide détour to Habsheim where the Germans have an aviation field, but all to no avail. Not a Boche was in the air.

The news of Rockwell's death was telephoned to the escadrille. The captain, lieutenant, and a couple of men jumped in a staff car and hastened to where he had fallen. On their return the American pilots were convened in a room of the hotel and the news was broken to them. With tears in his eyes the captain said: "The best and bravest of us all is no more."

No greater blow could have befallen the escadrille. Kiffin was its soul. He was loved and looked up to by not only every man in our flying corps but by every one who knew him. Kiffin was imbued with the spirit of the cause for which he fought and gave his heart and soul to the performance of his duty. He said: "I pay my part for Lafayette and Rochambeau," and he gave the fullest measure. The old flame of chivalry burned brightly in this boy's fine and sensitive being. With his death France lost one of her most valuable pilots. When he was over the lines the Germans did not pass—and he was over them most of the time. He brought down four enemy planes that were credited to him officially, and Lieutenant de Laage, who was his fighting partner, says he is convinced that Rockwell accounted for many others

KIFFIN ROCKWELL, OF ASHEVILLE, N. C.
Who was killed in an air duel over Verdun
"Kiffin was imbued with the spirit of the cause for which he fought. He
said: 'I pay my part for Lafayette and Rochambeau.'"

which fell too far within the German lines to be observed. Rockwell had been given the Médaille Militaire and the Croix de Guerre, on the ribbon of which he wore four palms, representing the four magnificent citations he had received in the order of the army. As a further reward for his excellent work he had been proposed for promotion from the grade of sergeant to that of second lieutenant. Unfortunately the official order did not arrive until a few days following his death.

The night before Rockwell was killed he had stated that if he were brought down he would like to be buried where he fell. It was impossible, however, to place him in a grave so near the trenches. His body was draped in a French flag and brought back to Luxeuil. He was given a funeral worthy of a general. His brother, Paul, who had fought in the Legion with him, and who had been rendered unfit for service by a wound, was granted permission to attend the obsequies. Pilots from all near-by camps flew over to render homage to Rockwell's remains. Every Frenchman in the aviation at Luxeuil marched behind the bier. The British pilots, followed by a detachment of five hundred of their men, were in line, and a battalion of French troops brought up the rear. As the slow moving procession of blue and khaki-clad men passed from the church to the graveyard, airplanes circled at a feeble height above and showered down myriads of flowers.

Rockwell's death urged the rest of the men to greater action, and the few who had machines were constantly after the Boches. Prince brought one down. Lufbery, the most skillful and successful fighter in the escadrille, would venture far into the enemy's lines and spiral down over a German aviation camp, daring the pilots to venture forth. One day he stirred them up, but as he was short of fuel he had to make for home before they took to the air. Prince was out in search of a combat at this time. He got it. He ran into the crowd Lufbery had aroused. Bullets cut into his machine and one exploding on the front edge of a lower wing broke it. Another shattered a supporting mast. It was a miracle that the machine did not give way. As badly battered as it was Prince succeeded in bringing it back from over Mulhouse, where the fight occurred, to his field at Luxeuil.

The same day that Prince was so nearly brought down Lufbery missed death by a very small margin. He had taken on more gasoline and made another sortie. When over the lines again he encountered a German with whom he had a fighting acquaintance. That is he and the Boche, who was an excellent pilot, had tried to kill each other on one or two occasions before. Each was too good for the other. Lufbery manoeuvred for position but, before he could shoot, the Teuton would evade him by a clever turn. They kept after one another, the Boche retreating into his lines. When they were nearing Habsheim, Lufbery glanced back and saw French shrapnel bursting over the trenches. It meant a German plane was over French territory and it was his duty to drive it off. Swooping down near his adversary he waved good-bye, the enemy pilot did likewise, and Lufbery whirred off to chase the other representative of Kultur. He caught up with him and dove to the attack, but he was surprised by a German he had not seen. Before he could escape three bullets entered his motor, two passed through the fur-lined combination he wore, another ripped open one of his woolen flying boots, his airplane was riddled from wing tip to wing tip, and other bullets cut the elevating plane. Had he not been an exceptional aviator he never would have brought safely to earth so badly damaged a machine. It was so thoroughly shot up that it was junked as being beyond repairs. Fortunately Lufbery was over French territory or his forced descent would have resulted in his being made prisoner.

I know of only one other airplane that was safely landed after receiving as heavy punishment as did Lufbery's. It was a two-place Nieuport piloted by a young Frenchman named Fontaine with whom I trained. He and his gunner attacked a German over the Bois le Pretre who dove rapidly far into his lines. Fontaine followed and in turn was attacked by three other Boches. He dropped to escape, they plunged after him forcing him lower. He looked and saw a German aviation field under him. He was by this time only 2,000 feet above the ground. Fontaine saw the mechanics rush out to grasp him, thinking he would land. The attacking airplanes had stopped shooting. Fontaine pulled on full power and headed for the lines. The German planes dropped down on him and again opened fire. They were on his level, behind and on his sides. Bullets whistled by him in streams. The rapid-fire gun on Fontaine's machine had jammed and he was helpless. His gunner fell forward on him, dead. The trenches were just ahead, but as he was slanting downward to gain speed he had lost a good deal of height, and was at only six hundred feet when he crossed the lines, from which he received a ground fire. The Germans gave up the chase and Fontaine landed with his dead gunner. His wings were so full of holes that they barely supported the machine in the air.

The uncertain wait at Luxeuil finally came to an end on the 12th of October. The afternoon of that day the British did not say: "Come on Yanks, let's call off the war and have tea," as was their wont, for the bombardment of Oberndorf was on. The British and French machines had been prepared. Just before climbing into their airplanes the pilots were given their orders. The English in their single-seated Sopwiths, which carried four bombs each, were the first to leave. The big French Brequets and Farmans then soared aloft with their tons of explosive destined for the Mauser works. The fighting machines, which were to convoy them as far as the Rhine, rapidly gained their height and circled above their charges. Four of the battleplanes were from the American escadrille. They were piloted respectively by Lieutenant de Laage, Lufbery, Norman Prince, and Masson.

The Germans were taken by surprise and as a result few of their machines were in the air. The bombardment fleet was attacked, however, and six of its planes shot down, some of them falling in flames. Baron, the famous French night bombarder, lost his life in one of the Farmans. Two Germans were brought down by machines they attacked and the four pilots from the American escadrille accounted for one each. Lieutenant de Laage shot down his Boche as it was attacking another French machine and Masson did likewise. Explaining it afterward he said: "All of a sudden I saw a Boche come in between me and a Breguet I was following. I just began to shoot, and darned if he didn't fall."

As the fuel capacity of a Nieuport allows but little more than two hours in the air the avions de chasse were forced to return to their own lines to take on more gasoline, while the bombardment planes continued on into Germany. The Sopwiths arrived first at Oberndorf. Dropping low over the Mauser works they discharged their bombs and headed homeward. All arrived, save one, whose pilot lost his way and came to earth in Switzerland. When the big machines got to Oberndorf they saw only flames and smoke where once the rifle factory stood. They unloaded their explosives on the burning mass.

The Nieuports having refilled their tanks went up to clear the air of Germans that might be hovering in wait for the returning raiders. Prince found one and promptly shot it down. Lufbery came upon three. He drove for one, making it drop below the others, then forcing a second to descend, attacked the one remaining above. The combat was short and at the end of it the German tumbled to earth. This made the fifth enemy machine which was officially credited to Lufbery. When a pilot has accounted for five Boches he is mentioned by name in the official communication, and is spoken of as an "Ace," which in French aerial slang means a super-pilot. Papers are allowed to call an "ace" by name, print his picture and give him a write-up. The successful aviator becomes a national hero. When Lufbery worked into this category the French papers made him a head liner. The American "Ace," with his string of medals, then came in for the ennuis of a matinee idol. The choicest bit in the collection was a letter from Wallingford, Conn., his home town, thanking him for putting it on the map.

Darkness was coming rapidly on but Prince and Lufbery remained in the air to protect the bombardment fleet. Just at nightfall Lufbery made for a small aviation field near the lines, known as Corcieux. Slow-moving machines, with great planing capacity, can be landed in the dark, but to try and feel for the ground in a Nieuport, which comes down at about a hundred miles an hour, is to court disaster. Ten minutes after Lufbery landed Prince decided to make for the field. He spiraled down through the night air and skimmed rapidly over the trees bordering the Corcieux field. In the dark he did not see a high-tension electric cable that was stretched just above the tree tops. The landing gear of his airplane struck it. The machine snapped forward and hit the ground on its nose. It turned over and over. The belt holding Prince broke and he was thrown far from the wrecked plane. Both of his legs were broken and he naturally suffered internal injuries. In spite of the terrific shock and his intense pain Prince did not lose consciousness. He even kept his presence of mind and gave orders to the men who had run to pick him up. Hearing the hum of a motor, and realizing a machine was in the air, Prince told them to light gasoline fires on the field. "You don't want another fellow to come down and break himself up the way I've done," he said.

Lufbery went with Prince to the hospital in Gerardmer. As the ambulance rolled along Prince sang to keep up his spirits. He spoke of getting well soon and returning to service. It was like Norman. He was always energetic about his flying. Even when he passed through the harrowing experience of having a wing shattered, the first thing he did on landing was to busy himself about getting another fitted in place and the next morning he was in the air again.

No one thought that Prince was mortally injured but the next day he went into a coma. A blood clot had formed on his brain. Captain Haff in command of the aviation groups of Luxeuil, accompanied by our officers, hastened to Gerardmer. Prince lying unconscious on his bed, was named a second lieutenant and decorated with the Legion of Honor. He already held the Médaille Militaire and Croix de Guerre. Norman Prince died on the 15th of October. He was brought back to Luxeuil and given a funeral similar to Rockwell's. It was hard to realize that poor old Norman had gone. He was the founder of the American escadrille and every one in it had come to rely on him. He never let his own spirits drop, and was always on hand with encouragement for the others. I do not think Prince minded going. He wanted to do his part before being killed, and he had more than done it. He had, day after day, freed the line of Germans, making it impossible for them to do their work, and three of them he had shot to earth.

Two days after Prince's death the escadrille received orders to leave for the Somme. The night before the departure the British gave the American pilots a farewell banquet and toasted them as their "Guardian Angels." They keenly appreciated the fact that four men from the American escadrille had brought down four Germans, and had cleared the way for their squadron returning from Oberndorf. When the train pulled out the next day the station platform was packed by khaki-clad pilots waving good-bye to their friends the "Yanks."

The escadrille passed through Paris on its way to the Somme front. The few members who had machines flew from Luxeuil to their new post. At Paris the pilots were reinforced by three other American boys who had completed their training. They were: Fred Prince, who ten months before had come over from Boston to serve in aviation with his brother Norman; Willis Haviland, of Chicago, who left the American Ambulance for the life of a birdman, and Bob Soubrian, of New York, who had been

SERGEANT LUFBERY
In one of the new Nieuports in which he convoyed the bombardment fleet
which attacked Oberndorf.
All the American flyers have an Indian head painted on their machines.

transferred from the Foreign Legion to the flying corps after being wounded in the Champagne offensive.

Before its arrival in the Somme the escadrille had always been quartered in towns and the life of the pilots was all that could be desired in the way of comforts. We had, as a result, come to believe that we would wage only a de luxe war, and were unprepared for any other sort of campaign. The introduction to the Somme was a rude awakening. Instead of being quartered in a villa or hotel, the pilots were directed to a portable barracks newly erected in a sea of mud.

It was set in a cluster of similar barns nine miles from the nearest town. A sieve was a watertight compartment in comparison with that elongated shed. The damp cold penetrated through every crack, chilling one to the bone. There were no blankets and until they were procured the pilots had to curl up in their flying clothes. There were no arrangements for cooking and the Americans depended on the other escadrilles for food. Eight fighting units were located at the same field and our ever-generous French comrades saw to it that no one went hungry.

Squadron Insignia of the Lafayette Escadrille

The thick mist, for which the Somme is famous, hung like a pall over the birdmen's nest dampening both the clothes and spirits of the men.

Something had to be done, so Thaw and Masson, who is our Chef de Popote (President of the Mess) obtained permission to go to Paris in one of our light trucks. They returned with cooking utensils, a stove, and other necessary things. All hands set to work and as a result life was made bearable. In fact I was surprised to find the quarters as good as they were when I rejoined the escadrille a couple of weeks after its arrival in the Somme. Outside of the cold, mud, and dampness it wasn't so bad. The barracks had been partitioned off into little rooms leaving a large space for a dining hall. The stove is set up there and all animate life from the lion cub to the pilots centre around its warming glow.

The eight escadrilles of fighting machines form a rather interesting colony. The large canvas hangars are surrounded by the house tents of their respective escadrilles; wooden barracks for the men and pilots are in close proximity, and sandwiched in between the encampments of the various units are the tents where the commanding officers hold forth. In addition there is a bath house where one may go and freeze while a tiny stream of hot water trickles down one's shivering form. Another shack houses the power plant which generates electric light for the tents and barracks, and in one very popular canvas is located the community bar, the profits from which go to the Red Cross.

We had never before been grouped with as many other fighting escadrilles, nor at a field so near the front. We sensed the war to better advantage than at Luxeuil or Bar-le-Duc. When there is activity on the lines the rumble of heavy artillery reaches us in a heavy volume of sound. From the field one can see the line of sausage-shaped observation balloons, which delineate the front, and beyond them the high-flying airplanes, darting like swallows in the shrapnel puffs of anti-air-craft fire. The roar of motors that are being tested, is punctuated by the staccato barking of machine guns, and at intervals the hollow whistling sound of a fast plane diving to earth is added to this symphony of war notes.

CHAPTER III

PERSONAL LETTERS FROM SERGEANT MCCONNELL — AT THE FRONT

We're still waiting for our machines. In the meantime the Boches sail gaily over and drop bombs. One of our drivers has been killed and five wounded so far but we'll put a stop to it soon. The machines have left and are due to-day.

You ask me what my work will be and how my machine is armed. First of all I mount an avion de chasse and am supposed to shoot down Boches or keep them away from over our lines. I do not do observation, or regulating of artillery fire. These are handled by escadrilles equipped with bigger machines. I mount at daybreak over the lines; stay at from 11,000 to 15,000 feet and wait for the sight of an enemy plane. It may be a bombardment machine, a regulator of fire, an observer, or an avion de chasse looking for me. Whatever she is I make for her and manoeuvre for position. All the machines carry different gun positions and one seeks the blind side. Having obtained the proper position one turns down or up, whichever the case may be, and, when within fifty yards, opens up with the machine gun. That is on the upper plane and it is sighted by a series of holes and cross webs. As one is passing at a terrific rate there is not time for many shots, so, unless wounded or one's machine is injured by the first try—for the enemy plane shoots, too—one tries it again and again until there's nothing doing or the other fellow is dropped. Apart from work over the lines, which is comparatively calm, there is the job of convoying bombardment machines. That is the rotten task. The captain has called on us to act as guards on the next trip. You see we are like torpedo boats of the air with our swift machines.

We have the honour of being attached to a bombardment squadron that is the most famous in the French Army. The captain of the unit once lost his whole escadrille, and on the last trip eight lost their lives. It was a wonderful fight. The squadron was attacked by thirty-three Boches. Two French planes crashed to earth—then two German; another German was set on fire and streaked down, followed by a streaming column of smoke. Another Frenchman fell; another German; and then a French lieutenant, mortally wounded and realizing that he was dying, plunged his airplane into a German below him and both fell to earth like stones.

The tours of Alsace and the Vosges that we have made, to look over possible landing places, were wonderful. I've never seen such ravishing sights, and in regarding the beauty of the country I have missed noting the landing places. The valleys are marvellous. On each side the mountain slopes are a solid mass of giant pines and down these avenues of green tumble myriads of glittering cascades which form into sparkling streams beneath. It is a pleasant feeling to go into Alsace and realize that one is touring over country we have taken from the Germans. It's a treat to go by auto that way. In the air, you know, one feels detached from all below. It's a different world, that has no particular meaning, and besides, it all looks flat and of a weary pattern.

THE FIRST TRIP

Well, I've made my first trip over the lines and proved a few things to myself. First, I can stand high altitudes. I had never been higher than 7,000 feet before, nor had I flown more than an hour. On my trip to Germany I went to 14,000 feet and was in the air for two hours. I wore the fur head-to-foot combination they give one and paper gloves under the fur ones you sent me. I was not cold. In a way it seemed amusing to be going out knowing as little as I do. My mitrailleuse had been mounted the night before. I had never fired it, nor did I know the country at all even though I'd motored along our lines. I followed the others or I surely should have been lost. I shall have to make special trips to study the land and be able to make it out from my map which I carry on board. For one thing the weather was hazy and clouds obscured the view.

We left en escadrille, at 30-second intervals, at 6:30 a.m. I'd been on guard since three, waiting for an enemy plane. I climbed to 3,500 feet in four minutes and so started off higher than the rest. I lost them immediately but took a compass course in the direction we were headed. Clouds were below me and I could see the earth only in spots. Ahead was a great barrier of clouds and fog. It seemed like a limitless ocean. To the south the Alps jutted up through the clouds and glistened like icebergs in the morning sun. I began to feel completely lost. I was at 7,000 feet and that was all I knew. Suddenly I saw a little black speck pop out of a cloud to my left—then two others. They were our machines and from then on I never let them get out of my sight. I went to 14,000 in order to be able to keep them well in view below me. We went over Belfort which I recognized, and, turning, went toward the lines. The clouds had dispersed by this time. Alsace was below us and in the distance I could see the straight course of the Rhine. It looked very small. I looked down and saw the trenches and when I next looked for our machines I saw clusters of smoke puffs. We were being fired at. One machine just under me seemed to be in the centre of a lot of shrapnel. The puffs were white, or black, or green, depending on the size of the shell used. It struck me as more amusing than anything else to watch the explosions and smoke. I thought of what a lot of money we were making the Germans spend. It is not often that they hit. The day before one of our machines had a part of the tail shot away and the propeller nicked, but that's just bum luck. Two shells went off just at my height and in a way

A Nieuport 16 fighter with air to air rockets for attack on balloons.
The pilot is Charles Chouteau Johnson.

that led me to think that the third one would get me; but it didn't. It's hard even for the aviator to tell how far off they are. We went over Mulhouse and to the north. Then we sailed south and turned over the lines on the way home. I was very tired after the flight but it was because I was not used to it and it was a strain on me keeping a look-out for the others.

AT VERDUN

To-day the army moving picture outfit took pictures of us. We had a big show. Thirty bombardment planes went off like clock-work and we followed. We circled and swooped down by the camera. We were taken in groups, then individually, in flying togs, and God knows what-all. They will be shown in the States.

If you happen to see them you will recognize my machine by the MAC, painted on the side.

Seems quite an important thing to have one's own airplane with two mechanics to take care of it, to help one dress for flights, and to obey orders. A pilot of no matter what grade is like an officer in any other arm.

We didn't see any Boche planes on our trip. We were too

*Longueval after the British had recovered it for France: July 14th 1916
saw the beginning of the second stage of the great Battle of the Somme, and
on that day the British Troops penetrated into the German second line,
capturing Longueval, Bazentin-le-Grand, and Bazentin-le-Petit in their
stride. (Official British military photograph)*

many. The only way to do is to sneak up on them.

I do not get a chance to see much of the biggest battle in the
world which is being fought here, for I'm on a fighting machine
and the sky is my province. We fly so high that ground details
are lacking. Where the battle has raged there is a broad, browned
band. It is a great strip of murdered Nature. Trees, houses, and
even roads have been blasted completely away. The shell holes
are so numerous that they blend into one another and cannot be
separately seen. It looks as if shells fell by the thousand every
second. There are spurts of smoke at nearly every foot of the
brown areas and a thick pall of mist covers it all. There are but
holes where the trenches ran, and when one thinks of the poor
devils crouching in their inadequate shelters under such a

hurricane of flying metal, it increases one's respect for the staying powers of modern man. It's terrible to watch, and I feel sad every time I look down. The only shooting we hear is the tut-tut-tut of our own or enemy plane's machine guns when fighting is at close quarters. The Germans shoot explosive bullets from theirs. I must admit that they have an excellent air fleet even if they do not fight decently.

I'm a sergeant now—sergent in French—and I get about two francs more a day and wear a gold band on my cap, which makes old territorials think I'm an officer and occasions salutes which are some bother.

A SORTIE

We made a foolish sortie this morning. Only five of us went, the others remaining in bed thinking the weather was too bad. It was. When at only 3,000 feet we hit a solid layer of clouds, and when we had passed through, we couldn't see anything but a shimmering field of white. Above were the bright sun and the blue sky, but how we were in regard to the earth no one knew. Fortunately the clouds had a big hole in them at one point and the whole mass was moving toward the lines. By circling, climbing, and dropping we stayed above the hole, and, when over the trenches, worked into it, ready to fall on the Boches. It's a stunt they use, too. We finally found ourselves 20 kilometres in the German lines. In coming back I steered by compass and then when I thought I was near the field I dived and found myself not so far off, having the field in view. In the clouds it shakes terribly and one feels as if one were in a canoe on a rough sea.

VICTOR CHAPMAN

I was mighty sorry to see old Victor Chapman go. He was one of the finest men I've ever known. He was too brave if anything. He was exceptionally well educated, had a fine brain, and a heart as big as a house. Why, on the day of his fatal trip, he had put oranges in his machine to take to Balsley who was lying wounded with an explosive bullet. He was going to land near the hospital after the sortie.

Received letter inclosing note from Chapman's father. I'm glad you wrote him. I feel sure that some of my letters never reach you. I never let more than a week go by without writing. Maybe I do not get all yours, either.

A SMASH-UP

Weather has been fine and we've been doing a lot of work. Our Lieutenant de Laage de Mieux, brought down a Boche. I had another beautiful smash-up. Prince and I had stayed too long over the lines. Important day as an attack was going on. It was getting dark and we could see the tiny balls of fire the infantry light to show the low-flying observation machines their new positions. On my return, when I was over another aviation field, my motor broke. I made for field. In the darkness I couldn't judge my distance well, and went too far. At the edge of the field there were trees, and beyond, a deep cut where a road ran. I was skimming ground at a hundred miles an hour and heading for the trees. I saw soldiers running to be in at the finish and I thought to myself that James's hash was cooked, but I went between two trees and ended up head on against the opposite bank of the road. My motor took the shock and my belt held me. As my tail went up it was cut in two by some very low 'phone wires. I wasn't even bruised. Took dinner with the officers there who gave me a car to go home in afterward.

FIGHTING A BOCHE

To-day I shared another chap's machine (Hill of Peekskill), and got it shot up for him. De Laage (our lieutenant) and I made a sortie at noon. When over the German lines, near CÃ´te 304, I saw two Boches under me. I picked out the rear chap and dived. Fired a few shots and then tried to get under his tail and hit him from there. I missed, and bobbed up alongside of him. Fine for the Boche, but rotten for me! I could see his gunner working the mitrailleuse for fair, and felt his bullets darn close. I dived, for I could not shoot from that position, and beat it. He kept plunking away and altogether put seven holes in my machine. One was only ten inches in from me. De Laage was too far off to get to the Boche and ruin him while I was amusing him.

Yesterday I motored up to an aviation camp to see a Boche machine that had been forced to land and was captured. On the way up I passed a cantonment of Senegalese. About twenty of 'em jumped up from the bench they were sitting on and gave me the hell of a salute. Thought I was a general because I was riding in a car, I guess. They're the blackest niggers you ever saw. Good-looking soldiers. Can't stand shelling but they're good on the cold steel end of the game. The Boche machine was a beauty. Its motor is excellent and she carries a machine gun aft and one forward. Same kind of a machine I attacked to-day. The German pilots must be mighty cold-footed, for if the Frenchmen had airplanes like that they surely would raise the devil with the Boches.

As it is the Boches keep well within their lines, save occasionally, and we have to go over and fight them there.

KIFFIN ROCKWELL

Poor Kiffin Rockwell has been killed. He was known and admired far and wide, and he was accorded extraordinary honours. Fifty English pilots and eight hundred aviation men from the British unit in the Vosges marched at his funeral. There was a regiment of Territorials and a battalion of Colonial troops in addition to the hundreds of French pilots and aviation men. Captain Thénault of the American Escadrille delivered an exceptionally eulogistic funeral oration. He spoke at length of Rockwell's ideals and his magnificent work. He told of his combats. "When Rockwell was on the lines," he said, "no German passed, but on the contrary was forced to seek a refuge on the ground."

Rockwell made the esprit of the escadrille, and the Captain voiced the sentiments of us all when, in announcing his death, he said: "The best and bravest of us all is no more."

How does the war look to you—as regards duration? We are figuring on about ten more months, but then it may be ten more years. Of late things are much brighter and one can feel a certain elation in the air. Victory, before, was a sort of academic certainty; now, it's felt.

CHAPTER IV

HOW FRANCE TRAINS PILOT AVIATORS

France now has thousands of men training to become military aviators, and the flying schools, of which there is a very great number, are turning out pilots at an astounding rate.

The process of training a man to be a pilot aviator naturally varies in accordance with the type of machine on which he takes his first instruction, and so the methods of the various schools depend on the apparatus upon which they teach an élève pilote—as an embryonic aviator is called—to fly.

In the case of the larger biplanes, a student goes up in a dual-control airplane, accompanied by an old pilot, who, after first taking him on many short trips, then allows him part, and later full, control, and who immediately corrects any false moves made by him. After that, short, straight line flights are made alone in a smaller-powered machine by the student, and, following that, the training goes on by degrees to the point where a certain mastery of the apparatus is attained. Then follows the prescribed "stunts" and voyages necessary to obtain the military brevet.

TRAINING FOR PURSUIT AIRPLANES

The method of training a pilot for a small, fast avion de chasse, as a fighting airplane is termed, is quite different, and as it is the most thorough and interesting I will take that course up in greater detail.

The man who trains for one of these machines never has the advantage of going first into the air in a double-control airplane. He is alone when he first leaves the earth, and so the training preparatory to that stage is very carefully planned to teach a man the habit of control in such a way that all the essential movements will come naturally when he first finds himself face to face with the new problems the air has set for him. In this preparatory training a great deal of weeding out is effected, for a man's aptitude for the work shows up, and unless he is by nature especially well fitted he is transferred to the division which teaches one to fly the larger and safer machines.

First of all, the student is put on what is called a roller. It is a low-powered machine with very small wings. It is strongly built to stand the rough wear it gets, and no matter how much one might try it could not leave the ground. The apparatus is jokingly and universally known as a Penguin, both because of its humorous resemblance to the quaint arctic birds and its inability in common with them to do any flying. A student makes a few trips up and down the field in a double-control Penguin, and learns how to steer with his feet. Then he gets into a single-seated one and, while the rapidly whirling propeller is pulling him along, tries to keep the Penguin in a straight line. The slightest mistake or delayed movement will send the machine skidding off to the right or left, and sometimes, if the motor is not stopped in time, over on its side or back. Something is always being broken on a Penguin, and so a reserve flock is kept at the side of the field in order that no time may be lost.

After one is able to keep a fairly straight line, he is put on a Penguin that moves at a faster rate, and after being able to handle it successfully passes to a very speedy one, known as the "rapid." Here one learns to keep the tail of the machine at a proper angle by means of the elevating lever, and to make a perfectly straight line. When this has been accomplished and the monitor is thoroughly convinced that the student is absolutely certain of making no mistakes in guiding with his feet, the young aviator is passed on to the class which teaches him how to leave the ground. As one passes from one machine to another one finds

Victor Chapman, of New York City, of the French Flying Service, who was killed flying for France

that the foot movements must be made smaller and smaller. The increased speed makes the machine more and more responsive to the rudder, and as a result the foot movements become so gentle when one gets into the air that they must come instinctively.

FIRST FLIGHTS ALONE

The class where one will leave the ground has now been reached, and an outfit of leather clothes and casque is given to the would-be pilot. The machines used at this stage are low-powered monoplanes of the Blériot type, which, though being capable of leaving the ground, cannot rise more than a few feet. They do not run when the wind is blowing or when there are any movements of air from the ground, for though a great deal of balancing is done by correcting with the rudder, the student knows nothing of maintaining the lateral stability, and if caught in the air by a bad movement would be apt to sustain a severe accident. He has now only to learn how to take the machine off

A plane crash on a World War I training flight, likely a Curtiss JN-4.

the ground and hold it at a low line of flight for a few moments.

For the first time one is strapped into the seat of the machine, and this continues to be the case from this point on. The motor is started, and one begins to roll swiftly along the ground. The tail is brought to an angle slightly above a straight line. Then one sits tight and waits. Suddenly the motion seems softer, the motor does not roar so loudly, and the ground is slipping away. The class standing at the end of the line looks far below; the individuals are very small, but though you imagine you are going too high, you must not push to go down more than the smallest fraction, or the machine will dive and smash. The small push has brought you down with a bump from a seemingly great height. In reality you have been but three feet off the ground. Little by little the student becomes accustomed to leaving the ground, for these short hop-skip-and-jump flights, and has learned how to steer in the air.

If he has no bad smash-ups he is passed on to a class where

he rises higher, and is taught the rudiments of landing. If, after a few days, that act is reasonably performed and the young pilot does not land too hard, he is passed to the class where he goes about sixty feet high, maintains his line of flight for five or six minutes and learns to make a good landing from that height. He must by this time be able to keep his machine on the line of flight without dipping and rising, and the landings must be uniformly good. The instructor takes a great deal of time showing the student the proper line of descent, for the landings must be perfect before he can pass on.

Now comes the class where the pilot rises three or four hundred feet high and travels for more than two miles in a straight line. Here he is taught how to combat air movements and maintain lateral stability. All the flying up to this point has been done in a straight line, but now comes the class where one is taught to turn. Machines in this division are almost as high powered as a regular flying machine, and can easily climb to two thousand feet. The turn is at first very wide, and then, as the student becomes more confident, it is done more quickly, and while the machine leans at an angle that would frighten one if the training in turning had not been gradual. When the pilot can make reasonably close right and left turns, he is told to make figure eights. After doing this well he is sent to the real flying machines.

There is nothing in the way of a radical step from the turns and figure eights to the real flying machines. It is a question of becoming at ease in the better and faster airplanes taking greater altitudes, making little trips, perfecting landings, and mastering all the movements of correction that one is forced to make. Finally one is taught how to shut off and start one's motor again in the air, and then to go to a certain height, shut off the motor, make a half-turn while dropping and start the motor again. After this, one climbs to about two thousand feet and, shutting off the motor, spirals down to within five hundred feet of the ground.

When that has been practised sufficiently, a registering altitude meter is strapped to the pilot's back and he essays the official spiral, in which one must spiral all the way to earth with the motor off, and come to a stop within a few yards of a fixed point on the aviation grounds. After this, the student passes to the voyage machines, which are of almost twice the power of the machine used for the short trips and spirals.

TESTS FOR THE MILITARY BREVET

There are three voyages to make. Two consist in going to designated towns an hour or so distant and returning. The third voyage is a triangle. A landing is made at one point and the other two points are only necessary to cross. In addition, there are two altitudes of about seven thousand feet each that one has to attain either while on the voyages or afterward.

The young pilot has not, up to this point, had any experience on trips, and there is always a sense of adventure in starting out over unknown country with only a roller map to guide one and the gauges and controls, which need constant attention, to distract one from the reading of the chart. Then, too, it is the first time that the student has flown free and at a great height over the earth, and his sense of exultation at navigating at will the boundless sky causes him to imagine he is a real pilot. True it is that when the voyages and altitudes are over, and his examinations in aeronautical sciences passed, the student becomes officially a pilote-aviateur, and he can wear two little gold-woven wings on his collar to designate his capacity, and carry a winged propeller emblem on his arm, but he is not ready for the difficult work of the front, and before he has time to enjoy more than a few days' rest he is sent to a school of perfectionnement. There the real, serious and thorough training begins.

Schools where the pilots are trained on the modern machines—écoles de perfectionnement as they are called—are usually an annex to the centres where the soldiers are taught to fly, though there are one or two camps that are devoted exclusively to giving advanced instruction to aviators who are to fly the avions de chasse, or fighting machines. When the aviator enters one of these schools he is a breveted pilot, and he is allowed a little more freedom than he enjoyed during the time he was learning to fly.

He now takes up the Morane monoplane. It is interesting to note that the German Fokker is practically a copy of this machine. After flying for a while on a low-powered Morane and having mastered the landing, the pilot is put on a new, higher-powered model of the same make. He has a good many hours of flying, but his trips are very short, for the whole idea is to familiarize one with the method of landing. The Blériot has a landing gear that is elastic in action, and it is easy to bring to earth. The Nieuport and other makes of small, fast machines for which the pilot is training have a solid wheel base, and good landings are much more difficult to make. The Morane pilot has the same practices climbing to small altitudes around eight thousand feet and picking his landing from that height with motor off. When he becomes proficient in flying the single- and double-plane types he leaves the school for another, where shooting with machine guns is taught.

This course in shooting familiarizes one with various makes of machine guns used on airplanes, and one learns to shoot at targets from the air. After two or three weeks the pilot is sent to another school of combat.

TRICK FLYING AND DOING STUNTS

These schools of combat are connected with the écoles de perfectionnement with which the pilot has finished. In the combat school he learns battle tactics, how to fight singly and in fleet formation, and how to extract himself from a too dangerous position. Trips are made in squadron formation and sham battles are effected with other escadrilles, as the smallest unit of an aerial fleet is called. For the first time the pilot is allowed to do fancy flying. He is taught how to loop the loop, slide on his wings or tail, go into corkscrews and, more important, to get out of them, and is encouraged to try new stunts.

Finally the pilot is considered well enough trained to be sent to the reserve, where he waits his call to the front. At the reserve he flies to keep his hand in, practises on any new make of machine that happens to come out or that he may be put on in place of the Nieuport, and receives information regarding old and new makes of enemy airplanes.

At last the pilot receives his call to the front, where he takes his place in some established or newly formed escadrille. He is given a new machine from the nearest airplane reserve centre, and he then begins his active service in the war, which, if he survives the course, is the best school of them all.

CHAPTER V
AGAINST ODDS

Since the publication of previous editions of "Flying for France" we have obtained the following letters which add greatly to the interest and complete the record of McConnell's connection with the Lafayette Escadrille.

March 19, 1917.

DEAR PAUL:

We are passing through some very interesting times. The boches are in full retreat, offering very little resistance to the English and French advance. The boches have systematically destroyed all the towns and villages abandoned. Where they haven't burned a house, they have made holes through the roofs with pickaxes. All the cross-roads are blown up at the junctions, and when the trees bordering the roads haven't been cut down, barricading the roads, they have been cut half way through so that when the wind blows they keep falling on the passing convoys. The inhabitants left in these villages are wild with delight and are giving the troops an inspiring reception. In one town the boches raped all the women before leaving, then locked them down cellar, and carried off all the young girls with them.

We have been flying low, and watching the cavalry overrunning the country. The boches are retreating to very strongly fortified positions, where the advance is going to come up against a stone wall.

This morning Genet and McConnell flew well ahead of the advancing army, Mac leading. Genet saw two boche planes maneuvering to get above them, so he began to climb, too. Finally they got together; the boche was a biplane and had the edge on Genet. Almost the first shot got Genet in the cheek. Fortunately it was only a deep flesh wound, and another shot almost broke the stanchion, which supports the wings, in two. Genet stuck to the boche and opened fire on him. He knows he hit the machine and at one time he thought he saw the machine on fire, but nothing happened. At last the boche had Genet in a bad position, so he (Genet) piqued down about a thousand meters and got away from the boche. He looked around for Mac but couldn't find him, so he came home. Mac hasn't yet shown up and we are frightfully worried. Genet has a dim recollection that when he attacked the boche, the other boche piqued down in Mac's direction, and it looks as if the boche got Mac unawares. Late this afternoon we got a report that this morning a Nieuport was seen to land near Tergnier, which is unfortunately still in German hands. This must have been Mac's, in which case he is only wounded, or perhaps only his machine was badly damaged. There is a general feeling among us that Mac is all right. The French cavalry are within ten or fifteen kilometers of Tergnier now and perhaps they will take the place to-morrow, in which case we will certainly learn something. This afternoon Lieut. de Laage and Lufbery landed at Ham, where the advance infantry were, and made a lot of inquiries. It was near this place where the fight started. Nobody had seen any machine come down. You may be sure I will keep you informed of everything that turns up. Genet is going to write you in a day or so.

Sincerely,

WALTER (signed Walter Lovell).

P. S. I apologize for the mistakes and the disconnectedness of this letter, but I wrote it in frightful haste in order to get it in the first post.

March 20, 1917.

MY DEAR ROCKWELL:

I do not know if any of the boys have written you about the

disappearance of Jim, so perhaps you might know something about it when this letter reaches you.

He left yesterday at 8:45 a.m. in his machine for the German lines, and has not returned yet. He and Genet were attacked by two Germans, the latter, who received a slight wound on the cheek, was so occupied he did not see what became of Jim, and returned without him.

The combat took place between Ham and St. Quentin; the territory was still occupied by the enemy when the combat took place. The worst I hope has happened to our friend is that perhaps he was wounded and was forced to land in the enemy's lines and was made prisoner. Nothing definite is known. I shall write you immediately I get news.

I am extremely worried. To lose my friend would be a severe blow. I can't and will not believe that anything serious has happened.

Best wishes,

Sincerely,

E. A. MARSHALL.

Escadrille N. 124, Secteur Postal 182, March 21, 1917.

MY DEAR PAUL:

Had I been feeling less distressed and miserable on Monday morning, or during yesterday, I would have written you then, but I told Lovell to tell you how I felt when he wrote on Monday and that I would try and write in a day or so. I am not feeling much better mentally but I'll try and write something, for I am the only one who was out with poor Mac on Monday morning and it just adds that much more to my distress.

As you know, we have had a big advance here, due to the deliberate evacuation by the Germans, without much opposition, of the territory now in the hands of the French and English. The advance began last Thursday night and each day has brought the lines closer to Saint Quentin and the region north and south of it.

On Monday morning Mac, Parsons, and myself went out at nine o'clock on the third patrol of the escadrille. We had orders to protect observation machines along the new lines around the region of Ham. Mac was leader. I came second and Parsons followed me. Before we had gone very far Parsons was forced to go back on account of motor trouble, which handicapped us greatly on account of what followed, but of course that cannot be remedied because Parsons was perfectly right in returning when his motor was not running well. We all do that one time or another.

Mac and I kept on and up to ten o'clock were circling around the region of Ham, watching out for the heavier machines doing reconnoitring work below us. We went higher than a thousand meters during that time. About ten, for some reason or other of his own, Mac suddenly headed into the German lines toward Saint Quentin and I naturally followed close to his rear and above him. Perhaps he wanted to make observations around Saint Quentin. At any rate, we had gotten north of Ham and quite inside the hostile lines, when I saw two boche machines crossing towards us from the region of Saint Quentin at an altitude quite higher than ours. We were then about 1,600 meters. I supposed Mac saw them the same as I did. One boche was much farther ahead than the other, and was headed as if he would dive at any moment on Mac. I glanced ahead at Mac and saw what direction he was taking, and then pulled back to climb up as quickly as possible to gain an advantageous height over the nearest boche. It was cloudy and misty and I had to keep my eyes on him all the time, so naturally I couldn't watch Mac. The second boche was still much farther off than his mate. By this time I had gotten to 2,200, the boche was almost up to me and taking a diagonal course right in front. He started to circle and his gunner—it was a biplane, probably an Albatross, although the mist was too thick

Bombsight on a World War I training flight.

and dark for me to see much but the bare outline of his dirty, dark green body, with white and black crosses—opened fire before I did and his first volley did some damage. One bullet cut the left central support of my upper wing in half, an explosive bullet cut in half the left guiding rod of the left aileron, and I was momentarily stunned by part of it which dug a nasty gouge into my left cheek. I had already opened fire and was driving straight for the boche with teeth set and my hand gripping the triggers making a veritable stream of fire spitting out of my gun at him, as I had incendiary bullets, it being my job lately to chase after observation balloons, and on Saturday morning I had also been up after the reported Zeppelins. I had to keep turning toward the boche every second, as he was circling around towards me and I was on the inside of the circle, so his gunner had all the advantage over me. I thought I had him on fire for one instant as I saw—or supposed I did—flames on his fuselage. Everything passed in a few seconds and we swung past each other in opposite directions at scarcely twenty-five meters from each other—the boche beating off towards the north and I immediately dived down in the opposite direction wondering every second whether the broken wing support would hold together or not and feeling weak and stunned from the hole in my face. A battery opened a heavy fire on me as I went down, the shells breaking just behind me. I straightened out over Ham at a thousand meters, and began to circle around to look for Mac or the other boche, but saw absolutely nothing the entire fifteen minutes I stayed there. I was fearful every minute that my whole top wing would come off, and I thought that possibly Mac had gotten around toward the west over our lines, missed me, and was already on his way back to camp. So I finally turned back for our camp, having to fly very low and against a strong northern wind, on account of low clouds just forming. I got back at a quarter to eleven and my first question to my mechanic was: "Has McConnell returned?"

He hadn't, Paul, and no news of any sort have we had of him yet, although we hoped and prayed every hour yesterday for some word to come in. The one hope that we have is that on account of this continued advance some news will be brought in of Mac through civilians who might have witnessed his flight over the lines north of Ham, while they were still in the hands of the enemy, for many of the civilians in the villages around there are being left by the Germans as they retire. We can likewise hope that Mac was merely forced to land inside the enemy lines on account of a badly damaged machine, or a bad wound, and is well but a prisoner. I wish to God, Paul, that I had been able to see Mac during his combat, or had been able to get down to him sooner and help him. The mists were thick, and consequently seeing far was difficult. I would have gone out that afternoon to look for him but my machine was so damaged it took until yesterday afternoon to be repaired. Lieut. de Laage and Lufbery did go out with their Spads and looked all around the region north of Ham towards Saint Quentin but saw nothing at all of a Nieuport on the ground, or anything else to give news of what had occurred.

The French are still not far enough towards Saint Quentin to be on the territory where the chances are Mac landed, so we'll still have to wait for to-day's developments for any possibility of news. I got lots of hope, Paul, that Mac is at least alive although undoubtedly a prisoner. I know how badly the news has affected you. We're all feeling mighty blue over it and as for myself—I'm feeling utterly miserable over the whole affair. Just as soon as any definite news comes in I'll surely let you know at once. Meanwhile, keep cheered and hopeful. There's no use in losing hope yet. If a prisoner Mac may even be able to escape and return to our lines, on account of the very unsettled state of the retreating Germans. Others have done so under much less favorable conditions.

I hope you are having a very enjoyable trip through the South. Walter showed me the postal you wrote him, which he received yesterday. Please give my very warm regards to your wife. Write as soon as you can, too.

Very faithfully yours,
EDMOND C. C. GENET.

March 22, 1917.

MY DEAR ROCKWELL:

Still no news about Jim. Last night the captain sent out a request to the military authorities to have our troops advancing in the direction of Saint Quentin report immediately any particulars about avion 2055. Even now I cannot reconcile myself concerning Jim's fate. I hope he has been made prisoner.

Just a few words about myself. I am awaiting the results of my friends' actions in the States on my behalf. I am placed in a peculiar position in the escadrille. I have nothing to do here. Shall I take care of Jim's belongings?

Best wishes,
Sincerely,
E. A. MARSHALL.

Escadrille N. 124, Secteur Postal 182, March 23, 1917.
DEAR PAUL:

In my letter I promised to send you word as soon as any definite news came in concerning poor Mac. To-day word came in from a group of French cavalry that they witnessed our fight on Monday morning and that they saw Mac brought down inside the German lines towards Saint Quentin after being attacked by two boche machines and at the same time they saw me fighting a third one higher than Mac, and that just as I piqued down Mac fell so there were three boche machines instead of two, as I supposed, having missed seeing the third one on account of the heavy clouds and mist around us.

There is still the hope that Mac wasn't killed but only wounded and a prisoner. If he is we'll learn of it later. The cavalrymen didn't say whether he came down normally or fell. Possibly he was too far off really to tell definitely about that. Certainly he had been already brought down before I could get down to help him after the boche I attacked beat it off. Had I known there were three boche machines I certainly would not have played around that boche at such a distance from Mac.

When will Mrs. Weeks return to Paris from the States? Will you write and tell her about Mac? She'll be mighty well grieved to hear of it, I know, and you'll be the best one to break it to her.

Write to me soon. Best regards to Mrs. Rockwell.
E. GENET.

March 24th, a. m. C. Aeronatique, Noyon & D. C. 13.
MY DEAR ROCKWELL:

The targe element informs us that it has found, in the environs of the Bois l'Abbe, a Nieuport No. 2055. The aviator, a sergeant, has been dead since three days, in the opinion of the doctor. His pockets appear to have been searched, for no papers were found on him. The Bois l'Abbe is two kilometers south of Jussy. The above message received by us at ten o'clock last night. Jussy is on the main road between Saint Quentin and Chauny. I expect to go back to the infantry soon.

Sincerely,

E. A. MARSHALL.

Escadrille N. 124, Secteur Postal 182, March 25, 1917.

DEAR PAUL:

The evening before last definite news was brought to us that a badly smashed Nieuport had been found by French troops, beside which was the body of a sergeant-pilot which had been there at least three days and had been stripped of all identification papers, flying clothes and even the boots. They got the number of the machine, which proved without further question that it was poor Mac. They gave the location as being at the little village of Petit Detroit, which is just south of Flavy-le-Martel, the latter place being about ten kilometers east of Ham on the railroad running from Ham to La Fere.

After having made a flight over the lines yesterday morning, I went down around Petit Detroit to locate the machine. There was no decent place there on which to land so I circled around over it for a few minutes to see in which condition it (the Nieuport) was. The machine was scarcely distinguishable so badly had it smashed into the ground, and there is scarcely any doubt, Paul, that Mac was killed while having his fight in the air, as no pilot would have attempted to land a machine in the tiny rotten field—no more than a little orchard beside the road— voluntarily. It seems almost certain that he struck the ground with full motor on. Captain Thénault landed some distance from there that he might go over there in a car and see just what could be done about poor Mac's body. When he returned last night he told us the following:

Mac, he said, was as badly mangled as the machine and had been relieved of his flying suit by the damned boches, also of his shoes and all papers. The machine had struck the ground so hard that it was half buried, the motor being totally in the earth and the rest, including even the machine gun, completely smashed. It was just beside the main road, in a small field containing apple trees cut down by the retreating boches, and just at the southern edge of the village.

Mac has been buried right there beside the road, and we will see that the grave is decently marked with a cross, etc. The captain brought back a square piece of canvas cut from one of the wings, and we are going to get a good picture we have of Mac enlarged and placed on this with a frame. I suppose that Thaw or Johnson will attend to the belongings of Mac which he had written are to be sent to you to care for. In the letter which he had left for just such an occasion as this he concludes with the following words: "Good luck to the rest of you. God damn Germany and vive la France!"

All honour to him, Paul. The world will look up to him, as well as France, for whom he died so gloriously, just as it is looking up to your fine brother and the rest of us who have given their lives so freely and gladly for this big cause.

Warmest regards, etc.,

Faithfully,

EDMOND C. C. GENET.

P. S. The captain has already put in a proposal for a citation for Mac, and also one for me. Mac surely deserved it, and lots more too.

German aviator dropping a bomb somewhere on the western front.

Escadrille N. 124, S. P. 182, March 27, 1917.
DEAR PAUL:

I got your postcard to-day and would have written you sooner about poor Jim but haven't been up to it, which I know you understand.

It hit me pretty hard, Paul, for as you know we were in school and college together, and for the last four or five years have been very intimate, living in N.C. and New York together.

It's hell, Paul, that all the good boys are being picked off. The damned Huns have raised hell with the old crowd, but I think we have given them more than we have received. The boys who have gone made the name for the escadrille and now it's up to us who are left (especially the old Verdun crowd) to keep her going and make the boches suffer.

Like old Kiffin, Mac died gloriously and in full action. It was in a fight with three Germans in their lines. Genet took one Hun (and was wounded). The last he saw was a Hun on Mac's back. Later we learned from the cavalry that there were two on Mac and after a desperate fight Mac crashed to the ground. This was the 19th of March. Three days later we took the territory Mac fell in and they were unable to distinguish who he was. The swine Huns had taken every paper or piece of identification from him and also robbed him—even took his shoes. The captain went over and was able to identify him by the number of his machine and uniform. He had lain out there three days and was smashed so terribly that you couldn't recognize his face. He was buried where he fell in a coffin made from the door of a pillaged house. His last resting place (and where he fell) is "Petit Detroit," which is a village southwest of Saint Quentin and north of Chauney. He is buried just at the southeast end of the village and in a hell of a small town.

Jim left a letter of which I am copying the important parts:

"In case of my death or made prisoner—which is worse—please send my canteen and what money I have

on me, or coming to me [he had none on him as the Huns lifted that] *to Mr. Paul A. Rockwell, 80 rue, etc. Shoes, tools, wearing apparel, etc., you can give away. The rest of my things, such as diary, photos, souvenirs, croix de guerre, best uniform* [he had best uniform on and I think the croix de guerre—however, you may find the latter in his things, his other uniform can't be found], *please put in canteen and ship along.*

"*Kindly cable my sister, Mrs. Followsbee, 65 Bellevue Place, Chicago. It would be kind to follow same by a letter telling about my death* [which I am doing].

"*I have a box trunk in Paris containing belongings I would like to send home. Paul R. knows about it and can attend to the shipping. I would appreciate it if the committee of the American Escad. would pay to Mr. Paul Rockwell the money needed to cover express.*

"*My burial is of no import. Make it as easy as possible for yourselves. I have no religion and do not care for any service. If the omission would embarrass you I presume I could stand the performance.* [Note Jim's keen sense of humour even to death instructions.]

"*Good luck to the rest of you. God damn Germany and vive la France.*

"*Signed,*

"*J. R. McCONNELL.*"

Jim had on the day of his death been proposed for the Croix de Guerre with palm. When it comes I shall send it to you.

Well, Paul, I have told you everything I can think of, but if there are any omissions or questions don't hesitate to ask.

I think we are now beginning to see the beginning of the end. The devastation, destruction and misery the Huns have left is a disgraceful crime to civilization and is pitiful. It drives me so furious I can't talk about it.

Best regards to you, old boy, and luck. All join in the above.

I shall wind up the same as Jim.

 As always,

 CHOUT (Charles Chouteau Johnson).

P. S. Steve Biglow is taking canteen to your place in Paris to-morrow, so you will find it there upon your return.

 C. J.

MORE FROM THE SAME SERIES

Most books from the 'Military History from Original Sources' series are edited and endorsed by Emmy Award winning film maker and military historian Bob Carruthers, producer of Discovery Channel's Line of Fire and Weapons of War and BBC's Both Sides of the Line. Long experience and strong editorial control gives the military history enthusiast the ability to buy with confidence. The series advisor is David McWhinnie, producer of the acclaimed Battlefield series for Discovery Channel. David and Bob have co-produced books and films with a wide variety of the UK's leading historians including Professor John Erickson and Dr David Chandler.
Where possible the books draw on rare primary sources to give the military enthusiast new insights into a fascinating subject.

The English Civil Wars   The Zulu Wars   Into Battle with Napoleon 1812   Waterloo 1815

The Anglo-Saxon Chronicle   Medieval Warfare   Renaissance Warfare   1914-1918

Sea Battles in the Age of Sail   Sun Tzu - The Art of War   Recollections of the Great War in the Air   Soldier of the Empire

For more information visit www.pen-and-sword.co.uk